CRYSTAL
BEGINNERS

Discover The Healing Power Of Crystals And Healing Stones To Heal The Human Energy Field, Relieve Stress and Experience Instant Relaxation.

L. Jordan

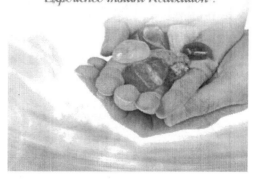

4th Edition

Free bonus inside this book

Table of Contents

Introduction

In a fast-paced world that causes suffering from imbalance and countless health maladies, we're typically offered the quickest solution to ease wellness issues: medication, either in the form of a prescription or an over-the-counter drug. Yet, filling ourselves up with harmful substances that present risks from serious side effects is hardly the best possible solution. Regardless of whether you're suffering from a bodily or mental imbalance, you're better off healing with a powerful and effective naturally-occurring resource: crystals.

In fact, you can use crystals to help balance your human energy field, also known as your chakras. If you're unfamiliar with the chakras, fear not: we'll explain all of this shortly. What you should know, however, is that you're about to embark on a healing journey that's perhaps deeper than any type of self-exploration you've ever considered before, and that the practices and restorative powers you'll learn about are long-lasting, effective, and rooted in the spiritual realm.

Of course, the role of nature in all this healing and life boosting process cannot be ignored. Crystals have natural energies flowing in them, some even associated with the satellites; the moon as well as the sun. And so they help you streamline your life, not only in matters of general health, but also in matters of love and romance. You will see from this book how possible it is to clear past hurts from relationships gone bad; how to begin a healthy love life; and even how to boost and strengthen your existing relationship. You will also be able to see the value of healing crystals in acting in place of medication, especially where medicating yourself would bring you life threatening side effects. Gladly, crystals are not just safe to the most vulnerable, like kids and expectant mothers;

they are also affordable to ordinary folk. Particularly if you consider that crystals are long lasting, their cost effectiveness will become obvious to you.

It is also gratifying to note that this book will show you how to use crystals to improve your financial situation; develop charisma; and neutralize the hatred of your foes. As such, what you will be looking forward to is nothing short of a happy and fulfilling future. Happy reading!

Chapter 1:
Are Crystals the Same as Gemstones?

Why would anyone wonder if crystals and gemstones refer to the same things? The confusion is easy to explain – when you enter a jewelry shop sometimes you hear gem and crystal being mentioned in the same breath. Reason...? Some crystals are gems but some gems are not crystals. Said differently, you can find gemstones that are just that and they will not help you to serve the purpose that a crystal does. On the contrary, many are those crystals which do what gemstones do – enhancing beauty.

And what is that purpose of a gem?

Basically, gemstones are for enhancing beauty. Sometimes too, because of their monetary value, they also make a statement as to what social status the wearer belongs. So in saying that some crystals can be gems means that some of them enhance beauty just as any other gemstone. And again, they happen to be pricey too.

In the making of gemstones, some expertise in cutting and polishing the stones is required. And the stones from which gems are cut are not those you are going to find easily. No wonder they are referred to as precious stones; some of them semi-precious.

When you want to talk of precious stones, think diamonds; emerald; ruby; and also sapphire. Those others are semi-precious. And what other fact do you learn here regarding gems? Of course, you learn that you can have gemstones that are actually of mineral nature – like diamonds.

Whereas gems and crystals are both sought after, what buyers look for in each of them is different. For gems, people are ready to part with hefty amounts, not just because the gem is rare, but also because of its color; how hard it is; its make-up; and how it has been cut.

What then is the uniqueness of crystals?

Did you know the word crystal is originally Greek? Well, the meaning over there is the substance you get after something coagulates through freezing; like ice. The word in Greek is *krustallos*, and the relationship in lexical structure both in English and Greek is unmistakable. On top of that you get the clear notion that crystals come about after a crystallization process.

The uniqueness of a crystal lies in how its atoms and molecules are arranged; in fact the unique arrangement begins right from the level of ions. Their arrangement is quite orderly and also appealing; creating a look of three distinct spatial dimensions. And because the make-up of crystals is pure elements, they usually emerge with flattering radiance. And the fact that light easily passes right through them enhances that radiance; effectively determining the color of the crystal. Mark you crystals develop over time so that one layer builds over another in the course of time.

Such crystallization of substances that results into this neat arrangement of molecules that radiates is what makes the crystals fall into the category of gemstones. Otherwise, if they do not have those attractive properties, then they will not fall into the category of gems; pieces that can be used for jewelry or such other adornment. Years ago, when someone mentioned a crystal, what came to mind was quartz. But today the list of crystals has become longer; with some pieces effectively being poly crystals, meaning that you get crystals interlinked somewhat symmetrically to form a kind of twin.

Differences in Pricing

It is easy to tell the price range to expect from jewelry considering they are made from gemstones, and that is because the mention of the mineral from which it is made gives it away. For instance, everyone knows how rare gold is and so anything gold made should, in our psyche, call for a big price.

What determines the price of a crystal?

Whereas how attractive a crystal looks could count as a determining factor, it is truly subjective, because as they say, beauty is in the individual's eye. However, there are factors that give pricing some consistency and they have been adopted from the four Cs used in gemstone pricing.

Carat

What size is the piece of crystal? What happens, for example, when you have some piece of jewelry is that it may have a body that is made from not-so-rare material, but have the piece of precious crystal right in the middle of it. That is, of course, the part that draws attention to the wearer and that is the piece whose carats determine the price. Carat is just a measure of precious material like gold, amber and so on. For simplicity, think of it as 200 milligrams; its equivalent in metric measurements. The more the carats, meaning the larger the precious crystal size, the higher the price.

Of course, if in the process of your crude explorations, you come across a crystal that nobody has documented before you can consider yourself lucky. You will have hit a jackpot because then the elements of rarity, newness and uniqueness would come in to influence the price – and push size to the periphery.

Clarity

How does light penetrate through the piece of crystal to give that mesmerizing radiance? If your piece is so transparent that light gets through it uninhibited from top to bottom, then you have got yourself a precious piece whose price will be just as high. On the contrary, you should expect a comparatively lower price for a crystal that has a good part of it milky and only a speck of clarity. It is on this basis that quartz crystals are relatively pricey.

Color

When it comes to color, the look combines with how much more attractive the crystal is than the milky ones. If its look gives it a higher aesthetic value, then price is bound to shoot. And if it adds rarity to it, you have a pricey piece. Such crystals that fit the bill are Arkansas Quartz crystals. These are not so easy to find and they look somehow smoky from the process of radiation. And that smoky look is captivating.

Condition

This is one of those Cs that is really not much consideration when it comes to valuing precious stones. Instead, the manner in which those ones have been cut comes into consideration.

Here, since you do not cut crystals but just collect those as they are naturally formed, what you consider is their state – their condition; including internal. Some may be all smooth and spotless while others may have visible cracks; even internally. The flawless ones will, obviously, be offered at a higher price. Some of those flaws occur while the crystals are still underground due to natural earth movement.

Chapter 2:
The Crystal Story

Crystals have a fascinating history. In fact, the best documentation of individuals, and not communities, letting their voice heard on the issue of crystals was in Germany. This need not surprise you if you consider that Germany is historically a religious country – meaning that believing in some power beyond human understanding is not alien to them.

As far as crystals are concerned, there was this court physician, Anselmus de Boot. He used to attend to Rudolf II who was the emperor of Germany in early 1600s. In 1609, this court physician pronounced that whether a crystal was valuable or not depended on whether it was occupied by good or bad angels. As far as he was concerned, good angels conferred special grace to those crystals that they occupied. On the other hand, bad angels made people believe that the crystals were powerful all on their own without any connection to divine powers. In short, people who made use of the bad crystals were simply superstitious. Of course, many people would wish to go for the good crystals that were considered helpful because of their divine connection.

Then along came Thomas Nichols in the same century and he began writing negative things about crystals and their limitations. According to this son of a physician from Cambridge, all the stuff about crystals being able to heal and impact your life positively was all baseless and untrue. Within the same period that Nichols was disputing the power of crystals, across Europe, the age of enlightenment was emerging and slowly but gradually, crystals were disqualified as anything helpful. They were said to be mere inanimate objects with no impact on anyone or on anything living.

But on the dawn of the 19th century, things on the crystal front were beginning to look up. Certain experiments were carried out and positive results were registered. In fact, positive impact was said to come particularly from individuals who claimed to have some clairvoyant abilities. There was one such person who confirmed experiencing emotional changes as well as physical ones once in contact with particular crystals. Those who vouched for crystals also claimed they registered varying smells when using crystals.

Daily use of crystals is pretty ancient

Come to think of it – who has not found a grandma or a mother wearing some ornament with stone-like pieces or some ring or bracelet, or even a necklace that looked like part of her than a piece of adornment? Even men have been known to wear studs of crystal if not hanging pendants around their necks. And even for those who have not had relatives wearing those, chances are you have seen some pieces of crystal decorations placed in strategic places in your home or a friend's home. You may not have attached much value to them then, but looking back you may identify some behavior or some aura that you can link to those pieces bringing tranquility into the home.

It is not easy to tell when exactly people began attaching much value to crystals, but it seems that this attachment is as ancient as people can remember. Crystals have been worn as talismans and others as amulets, although you cannot tell for sure if in those early centuries crystals had the exact same meaning as today.

What stood out, though, in early days, is that the crystals were kept pure. For instance, a gigantic piece of ivory was found in a place named Sungir in Russia when a grave was excavated. That piece was said to have been at least 60,000yrs old. Elsewhere, excavation of graves has revealed pieces of shell and even fossils of shark's teeth.

And then there is the Baltic amber that is seen to have existed as far back as 30,000 years ago. In fact, people must have had an extreme attachment to these crystals seeing that the Christian church found it necessary to ban their use in 355 AD.

Some countries that have evidence of ancient use of crystals

America

Why would it surprise anyone really? America is home to some ancient tribes who originated from the East, and with them came traditions usually associated with the orient. Here are some particular American communities that have valued crystals from ancient times:

The Cherokee

From time immemorial, there is no Cherokee family that did not have crystals in their homestead. The family would place such crystals in strategic locations so that you had some catching the sun's rays in the morning; others around noon; while others still caught the sun's rays in the evening. That meant that the family was in full protection 24/7, courtesy of the natural crystals. Do you notice the relationship between the crystals and the sun in terms of energy alliance? These ancient communities may not have learnt modern science but they surely knew something about what modern science claims to have discovered many years later.

Anyway, the Cherokee ensured they consulted their Morning Crystal to see what the day had in store for them; and they would check with the other crystals at different times in the day for further guidance.

And how did they handle those who ventured outside the homestead, you may wonder?

- Well, it was the norm for every Cherokee to wear some crystal in some concealed area of the body. So you were always protected wherever you ventured.

- The only people who were not required to keep their crystals concealed were two chiefs – the Red Chief and the White Chief.

In fact, their crystals were clearly displayed hanging around their necks. While the White Chief took care of people's spiritual needs and ensured there was harmony within the village, the Red Chief ensured that the Cherokee's external affairs were well taken care of. Crystals were taken by the Cherokee to have such potent power that if ever a chief was felled in battle, his large crystal would be retrieved by an assigned warrior and buried within the thick of a tree trunk. The logic was that once buried in the deep of the tree trunk, the crystal was safe from the enemy and there was no risk of the enemy getting it and using its power to the opponent's advantage. Just in case the Cherokee chief was felled in an area that had no such trees, the warrior would take the crystal and smash it into unusable debris.

The Cherokee used crystals for serious baptism too

If you thought that the baptism of submerging people in water began with Jesus of Nazareth, the Biblical Son of God, you better learn more about these Native Americans. They would place 7 large size crystals in a stream and then submerge their people in the moving water in a bid to cleanse and purify them.

The Catawba

This Native American tribe of Indian descent who lived on the South Eastern side of America also took crystal to be very valuable. They would use the quartz for arrowheads as well as spear points.

The Navajo

This Native American tribe that lived on the South Western side of America valued crystals.

- They had their medicine men using crystals to protect the community from disease and other ills

- They also used the obsidian as arrowheads and also as spear points

Britain

Ancient Britons valued and used crystals too.

- There were amber beads made into amulets discovered in Britain, and experts indicated they must have been in existence for at least 10,000 years. However, since Britain is not known to produce amber, it is believed that those beads must have come with people from Europe or elsewhere.

- Ancient Britons also used the moonstone to enhance fertility. In fact, families have been known to have a piece of jewelry with moonstones being handed over from one generation to the next in a bid to continue their lineage.

Switzerland and Belgium

Paleolithic gravesites here have produced jet beads; jet bracelets; and even jet necklaces. That is clear indication that the jet crystal was popular in those areas.

Areas around modern day Iraq

The Sumerians, for example, made use of crystals in their magic rituals.

Egypt

In Sinai, deposits of malachite are evident, with actual mines said to have existed even in 4,000 BC. Besides the malachite, other crystals were also in use within Egypt and for different purposes.

- Egyptians would use various crystals as jewelry and they included lapis lazuli; turquoise; carnelian; the emerald; and also the clear quartz. And you cannot afford to ignore the value attached to the lapis lazuri after Cleopatra, the beautiful Egyptian pharaoh, made it the crystal of her choice.

- They would also these same crystals as amulets – meaning as protective pieces to keep the wearer from harm's way.

- They also used them to maintain their health

- To remove any evil spirit from amongst them and to combat terror that was feared to loom at night, the Egyptians used two major crystals – the peridot as well as the topaz. In earlier days, however, these crystals went by the name chrysolite.

- Egyptians also knew how to use crystals to enhance beauty. Lead ore, also known as galena, for example, was converted to powder and then applied as eye shadow. That particular shadow went by the name *kohl*. Malachite also did a good job of enhancing beauty, primarily as eye shadow too.

- Something about the rubies – dancers in Egypt wore them at the navel with the sole intention of fostering their sex appeal.

- For those Egyptians intent on raising their level of intellect, they wore crystal laden crowns. Of course, that is indication that the Egyptians had some knowledge about the third eye, irrespective of how they described it.

- Ancient Egyptians used the green stones in general at burials – of course, jade included. In fact, this particular custom was taken up in Mexico in later years. And over the years, these green stones have been taken as pieces of good luck in New Zealand.

Greece

Ancient Greeks valued crystals so much that some names used today to refer to crystals have Greek influence. Of course, beginning with the generic term itself, crystal, you realize it is a direct derivation from its Greek equivalent, *Krustallos*, which means ice.

- Of particular reference, of course, was the clear quartz, which the Greek believed was solidified water that was set to remain solid forever.

- Amethyst is also derived from Greek where the word means 'not intoxicated'. Ancient Greeks believed that this piece of quartz that was of the violet variety could keep them from being drunk and from having hangover.

- The Greeks of old took the hematite crystal with a religious angle, associating this piece of iron ore with their god of war, Aries. Their soldiers would actually rub it onto their bodies as protection from injury during war. They believed that hematite cleared them of any vulnerability during those dangerous missions.

- Greek sailors wore different types of amulets to keep them safe while at sea.

China

Ancient China took jade as a very important crystal

- You can even identify it being represented in Chinese writing where some of the characters are designed as representations of jade beads.

- The Chinese also used jade to make chimes which were then used as musical instruments.

- There is evidence that approximately 1,000 years ago, ancient Chinese used jade to build armor which they, at times, donned their departed emperors as they buried them.

In fact, it is said that around the same time, in Mexico, jade masks were being made and used during burials as well.

- Ancient China also too jade to be a kidney healing crystal. And South America is said to have associated jade with the same healing power too.

- As far as the history of crystals go in China, as back as 5,000 years ago, it is believed the Chinese still viewed and used crystals for healing purposes. In fact, it is from this ancient practice that modern Chinese have borrowed to be able to practice acupuncture as well as pranic healing.

New Zealand

In New Zealand, the Maoris made jade pendants which the male folk wore and then handed over from one generation to the next. Those jade pendants were said to have been representing the spirit of their ancestors.

Japan

Ancient Japanese used crystals while practicing scrying, a practice that is close to looking into a crystal ball the way psychics do. The quartz was particularly used to signify the dragon's heart; and of course, the dragon is revered in Japan as an animal bearing wisdom as well as power. That is the reason many Japanese, even today, wear tattoos with dragons images.

Any word for the skeptics...?

How can you explain the fact that ancient communities from worlds apart used particular crystals for the same purpose? Coincidence...? Divine intervention...?

Think about the jade crystal

The Chinese took it to be a healer for issues of the kidney. Incidentally, that was the same belief that the Aztecs held. And the Mayan community too... And where do you find the Aztecs? Well, somewhere within Central Mexico. And where do you find the Mayan community? These ones you find in Latin America of the Guatemala, El Salvador and the like. And even if you were to consider where the Mayan community originated from, it is still way off from China; being some place between the Caribbean Sea and the Gulf of Mexico – the place referred to as the Yucatan Peninsula.

- Then in different parts of the world, when you listen to ancient stories, what you hear is turquoise being associated with strength and health as a matter of fact.

- In the same vein, when you listen to different parts of the world, you realize that most communities used jasper for the same purpose – not only to provide strength but also calm.

Chapter 3:
What are the Chakras and Why are they Important?

Perhaps you've heard someone utter the word "chakra" before - it certainly wouldn't be hard to believe, especially since it's been spoken across all different cultures since the eighth century. Also known as the Sanskrit word for "wheel," the word chakra refers to one of the seven different energy centers within or around the body. While most individuals recognize the seven main chakras, it's said that there are in fact thousands of minor chakras that make up the human energy field.

The way a person's energy field behaves is determined by the vibrations that manifest themselves across the body. These main energy sources are, in fact, each of those seven chakras. To visualize these chakras, picture a wheel-like vortex that spins in a circular motion. It creates a vacuum of sorts, drawing in any kind of energy that it becomes exposed to at the corresponding vibratory level.

The chakras draw in information from our surroundings, but that's not always necessarily beneficial to us. Virtually anything, from a specific color vibration to micro or ultraviolet rays, can be drawn in. Likewise, others' auras and moods can enter into our spinning wheels, which is why we sometimes seem to feel as though someone's attitude can "rub off" on us. Just as other individuals can have an effect on us, we, too, can emit energy from our own chakras.

Another principle related to chakras is the widely-held belief that each of the seven chakras is connected to our existence in various ways: the chakra is embedded within us on a mental, physical, emotional, and spiritual plane. Physically, the chakra corresponds with a specific gland or organ, thereby dictating the energy level of these and other body parts.

In other words, every single part of our bodies is connected to a specific chakra. They are aligned vertically along the spinal column, and each has its own vitality level. If there is a disturbance amongst one of the chakras, its vitality will be affected. Thus, every aspect of our chakras - physical, mental, spiritual, and emotional - is linked.

That's why it's so important to maintain a level balance amongst our chakras. An imbalance, while possibly leading to physical discomfort, can go much deeper, and even have a detrimental effect on our emotional and mental wellbeing. Although each chakra has its own independent level of vitality, it's certainly possible that one imbalanced chakra can have a negative effect not only on surrounding body parts, but neighboring chakras as well. Again, this effect can be realized on a variety of levels, and doesn't have to relate only to the bodily functions - it can seep into mental, emotional, and spiritual realms as well.

If you were unfamiliar with the chakra system in the first place, you might think that it's impossible that you can have any imbalances within an aspect of your existence that you didn't even know you had. Yet, it's entirely possible that there's some sort of imbalance you're experiencing that you didn't even know was there. A depleted source of energy, whether spiritual or physical, can be a result of imbalanced chakras.

Oftentimes, in today's ever-evolving society, we neglect to concentrate on our own wellbeing and the harmony that we must maintain within ourselves. Regardless of how healthy we aim to be, it's quite difficult to ignore pollution and other toxic impurities within our surroundings. These, along with other negative forces such as unpleasant thoughts, can all be taken in by our chakras.

You'd most likely be surprised to learn about all of the different physical and emotional imbalances that result from a lack of harmony amongst your chakras. Issues spanning from arthritis to lack of creativity can all be attributed to an imbalanced chakra. Later on, we'll discuss in greater detail all of the chakras and the effects of their imbalances.

While a doctor can recommend medication, procedures, or offer a prescription for the symptoms of imbalanced chakras, it's ultimately up to us to maintain harmony across all of our realms: spiritual, mentally, and bodily. When we achieve balance amongst these aspects of ourselves, we can regulate our energy levels and open the door for free-flowing communication between all elements of our existence.

In order to regulate these aspects of ourselves, we can use healing crystals to achieve proper vitality levels within our chakras. Although the practices of eating well, keeping a healthy mind, and exercising are certainly beneficial to a person's overall wellbeing, they are not enough to maintain healthy chakras. While your chakra systems function automatically, they can be regulated through the use of healing crystals.

Moving forward, we'll discuss the specific crystals you can use to hone in on the vitality levels of each chakra. Before we can do that, however, it's important to grasp the function and purpose of each chakra and their corresponding energy focuses. We'll delve deeper into the seven chakras in the next chapter.

Chapter 4:
The Seven Principle Chakras

As we mentioned above, it's widely believed that there are thousands of minor chakras that make up our composition, each of which has its own energy level and purpose. For now, we'll focus on the main seven so that you can gain an understanding of each one's specific purpose. Firstly, it's important to recognize the fact that each of the seven main chakras has a specific corresponding mental, spiritual, physical, or emotional state. The reason we seek a balance amongst our chakras is so that we can achieve harmony across our mind, body, and spirit. Many traditions hold great importance in achieving this harmony - it's what allows us to heal ourselves from the inside out, using a holistic and spiritual approach.

The seven chakras are as follows:

The crown chakra (also known as the seventh chakra)

The location for this chakra is at the top of one's head and corresponds with the pineal gland. In Sanskrit, it's known as the Sahasrara, and can allow you to reach your greatest potential by overcoming life's obstacles and liberating your spirit. The crown chakra emphasizes the importance of achieving transcendence by following your own spiritual path. Yoga practitioners may recognize the symbol for the crown chakra, which is also associated with the dissipating silence that follows "Om." This chakra also encourages the possibility of striving for perfection and developing a sense of cosmic consciousness. The colors violet and golden-white typically correspond with the crown chakra.

When your crown chakra is imbalanced, you may experience sensitivity to light or other aspects of your surroundings, such as noises. You may also be prone to depression and experience difficulty in learning new things. Likewise, you might feel frequently confused, especially when it comes to spiritual and religious thoughts. Individuals who are living with an imbalanced crown chakra may also carry prejudices with them. By regulating the vitality of this chakra, we allow ourselves to live mindfully, thereby fully trusting our intuition and staying present in the moment.

The third eye chakra (also known as the sixth chakra)

This chakra can be found between the eyebrows, or along the forehead. It helps you develop a sense of understanding by abolishing confusion and confronting illusions. The third eye, known as the Ajna in Sanskrit, can also inspire your unique visionary processes. In addition, the third eye chakra corresponds with the pituitary gland and is associated with the color indigo. It's said to promote spiritual awareness and intuition.

If your third eye chakra is imbalanced, you may experience headaches, sinus problems, and imbalanced hormones. This chakra can also affect vision and hearing. On an emotional level, you could be prone to moodiness if this chakra's vitality levels are off. You may also daydream too frequently and lack an ability to observe and learn from others. Your imagination can become exaggerated as well. When we regulate this chakra, we invite others to offer wisdom, and we can also develop a clear distinction between truth and illusion. This clarity allows us to see the big picture of things.

The throat chakra (also known as the fifth chakra)

Known as the Vishuddha in Sanksrit, the throat chakra promotes communication and is located at the throat or the base of the neck. It aligns with the thyroid gland. The throat chakra aims to create clarity and a sense of expression, in addition to diminishing one's feelings of timidity or self-consciousness. It can also help to achieve a sense of divine guidance. The color that corresponds with the throat chakra is blue.

The imbalanced throat chakra runs the risk of leading to a thyroid disorder, in addition throat problems. Laryngitis, sore throats, and ear infections are all bodily issues that stem from a poorly balanced throat chakra. In addition, jaw problems such as TMJ, and neck or shoulder pain, can also be a result of a problem with the throat chakra's vitality levels. On the other hand, lack of self-expression and verbal or written communication blocks can occur within the mental and emotional realms. Individuals with weakened throat chakras ma feel as if they lack control over their lives, or have a diminished sense of willpower. When we balance this chakra, we allow words to flow from us freely, and can maintain a truthful, firm form of communication. We also listen well and in return, let our voices be heard by others.

The heart chakra (also known as the fourth chakra)

The heart chakra corresponds with the thymus gland and is responsible for enhancing the circulation of energy. It's fittingly located in the center of your chest, and it can also promote the expression of love and empathy. This chakra is also responsible for driving out cruelty and feelings of anger. Additionally, the heart chakra seeks emotional balance and universal consciousness. The Sanskrit word for the heart chakra is Anahata. Green and pink are the colors that are typically associated with this chakra.

Serious physical issues can result from an imbalanced heart chakra. Some examples of these ailments include heart and lung diseases, issues with the lymphatic system, asthma, and shoulder or arm pains. On an emotional level, the heart chakra, when imbalanced, can lead to detrimental feelings such as obsession, jealousy, anger, bitterness, and fear of loneliness. Balancing this chakra is extremely beneficial, as it creates a long-lasting sense of love, joy, and appreciation. Likewise, we are better able to forgive and trust others, and the ability to love is fully developed.

The solar plexus chakra (also known as the third chakra)

Located halfway between the navel and the bottom of the sternum, the solar plexus chakra is responsible for regulating your metabolism and deterring stagnation. It corresponds with the pancreas, and its matching color is yellow. This chakra is known as the Manipura in Sanskrit. It's also known to foster intellect, personal power, and ambition.

Digestive problems typically occur when the solar plexus chakra is off-balance. Other serious issues, such as high blood pressure, diabetes, and liver dysfunction can develop as a result of a weakened solar plexus chakra. In addition, chronic fatigue is a typical symptom of an imbalanced solar plexus chakra, as well as pancreas, gallbladder, and colon issues. Emotionally, we may feel overly critical of ourselves, and lack confidence in our physical appearances when our solar plexus chakra is suffering. We fear rejection and criticism, and tend to have a shortage of personal power. Yet, once we balance this chakra, we can develop confidence and a sense of self-respect.

Then, we are able to accept ourselves fully and maintain a healthy sense of assertiveness.

The sacral chakra (also known as the second chakra)

This chakra is located within the abdomen and is called "Swadhisthana" in Sanskrit. It creates a healthy sensual desire and reduces the need for reliance on any kinds of artificial substitutes for pleasure. Thus, it corresponds with the gonad. It's also sometimes referred to as the "spleen" chakra. The corresponding colors for this chakra are orange and blue-green. The sacral chakra fosters creativity and is linked to reproduction; additionally, it is linked with healing properties.

Because the sacral chakra corresponds with the sexual organs, it is therefore not surprising that reproductive issues can occur when this chakra is imbalanced. We may also develop urinary problems, kidney issues, and experience lower back, hip, or pelvic pain. Also, we may struggle to commit fully in relationships or express our emotions effectively and fully. An imbalanced sacral chakra can also inhibit our ability to express creativity and sexuality, and hinders our playfulness. Likewise, you may succumb to addictions or experience a fear of betrayal. Once this chakra is balanced, however, you'll hone in on your creativity, become passionate, outgoing, and sexually healthy. You can also become more committed and develop an ability to take risks. When this chakra is balanced to its fullest potential, you'll be able to honor others effectively.

The root chakra (also known as the first chakra)

The root chakra establishes an enriching bond between your life and the natural world. Known as the Muladhara in Sanskrit, this chakra also helps to diminish the dehumanizing elements that present themselves within a fast-paced, undergrounded life in today's society. It also helps to promote physical energy, stability, and a strong will. This chakra is located at the base of the spine. It corresponds with the adrenal gland and correlates with the colors red and black.

When the root chakra is imbalanced, physical problems such as issues in the rectum, tailbone, and lower extremities can occur. Men may experience problems in the prostrate or reproductive organs. An unhealthy immune system, degenerative arthritis, sciatica, eating disorders, and constipation can also result from an imbalanced root chakra. It's also possible to develop an emotional imbalance when it comes to food, money, and shelter, and one's overall ability to continually provide life's necessities. When balanced, the root chakra allows individuals to feel supported and connected, and develops a sense of safety in the world. Overall, it becomes possible to achieve a sense of self-preservation.

Chapter 5:
Is Crystal Healing at Loggerheads with Religion?

Clearly, crystal healing is in no way at loggerheads with religion; not to those who are well informed. Ever given thought to the ornaments you found your grannies donning? Some you would never wear in a million years whereas some of them were really attractive. If you asked, they probably would have explained to you that there was more to those ornaments than accentuating beauty.

In fact, there is evidence of amber beads in Britain as long ago as 10,000yrs; and Baltic amber someplace else as long ago as 30,000yrs. And since amber does not originate in the British Isles, that tells you some people must have travelled with those beads; meaning that amber was still a hot commodity even in those olden days. If, for instance, you observe Greek ancient customs, you find them attaching special value to the mineral, iron, associating it with their god of war, by the name of Aries. And still as a crystal, hematite is still valued as great for stimulating your mind. In short, there has always been some special power associated with crystals in a healthy and protective way in all spheres of life.

Although Christianity came to disassociate itself with ornaments worn as charms in the 4th century, you still find Rennes' Bishop Marbodus giving the agate crystal a clean bill of health during the 11th century; going as far as saying that it brings you closer to God. And, in fact, those who are familiar with Christianity, and especially Catholicism, know about ecclesiastical rings. The Catholic Church had preference for Sapphire being the gem for those rings. And even today sapphire is a valued crystal.

Then whatever much or little you know about religion, you, obviously, know that most religions are against drunkenness. And if you check out the origin of the crystal, amethyst, you realize that it happens to be Greek for *not drunken*.Surely such examples should allay any fears you may have about going against the grain when you are a religious person interested in crystals.

Have you heard of birthstones?

These are valued stones that are believed to invite good luck. And how bad could they be if you find them mentioned in positive light in the Biblical Book of Exodus? The book alludes to each of the twelve tribes of Israel having its own birthstone to bring them much needed good luck as well as protection. There, the birthstones bearing their names are said to have lined up Aaron's breastplate. And Aaron was a High Priest. Do you know where those tribes emerged from – just to give you some overview? There were twelve sons of Jacob, son of Isaac, the old man who was son of Abraham and who is said to have died at 180yrs of age – yes, one hundred and eighty! Now, each of those great grandchildren of Abraham began his own tribe. And those happen to be the tribes whose birthstones are mentioned in the book of Exodus.

Then when you check out the Koran you find the information that the fourth heaven is made of the carbuncle – or garnet. And there are plenty more positive examples from other religions including Hindu; Jainism; and even Buddhism, showing the importance of crystals within religion.

Today you can safely speak of the universality of crystals. Many individuals, religious inclinations and cultures notwithstanding, have begun to embrace the positive impact that crystals bring into their lives through enhancing their inner energy flow in a unique way.

How about looking at birthstones from three perspectives: traditional; modern; and religious? Who has accepted what crystal for each month? (See table next page)

Month	Traditional	Modern	Old Testament
January	Garnet	Garnet	Jasper
February	Amethyst	Amethyst	Sapphire
March	Aquamarine; Bloodstone	Aquamarine	Chalcedony
April	Diamond	Diamond; Quartz	Emerald
May	Emerald	Emerald	Sardonyx
June	Pearl; Moonstone	Alexandrite	Sardonyx
July	Ruby	Ruby	Chrysolite
August	Peridot; Sardonyx	Peridot	Beryl
September	Beryl	Beryl	Topaz
October	Opal; Tourmaline	Tourmaline; Opal; Rose Zircon	Chrysoprase
November	Topaz	Golden/Yellow Topaz; Citrine	Bloodstone
December	Turquoise; Lapis Lazuli	Tanzanite; Blue Zircon; Turquoise	Amethyst

More crystal affirmations within religion:

Amber

If you read the Biblical Book of Ezekiel, you find Ezekiel the priest describing his vision whereby he was in the presence of things that shone like topaz; or like some Bible versions describe it, like amber. With that brightness, he felt the presence as well as glory of God. There is also a sense of sanctification there. And when you relate that to the Greek equivalent of amber, which is *elektron*, meaning sun, then you can see how acceptable it is to relate the amber crystal with natural energy.

In fact, Greek mythology provides another Divine angle as to why you should feel warmth emanating from the amber crystals. They say that Helios' son, Phaeton – and Helios happened to be the sun god – died from being struck by lightning. His sisters shed so many tears in grief and those in turn transformed to amber droplets. Amber is then tied not just to energy but also warmth of the heart and health. In fact, if you are in the process of recovery, say from illness or injury of sorts, amber is the crystal to have with you.

Amethyst

Of course, this is one of those crystals that represented one of Israel's tribes. And it continued to be worn by Cardinals long after that. It is very noticeable in Bishop's rings as well. And when you delve deeper into history, you realize that the crystal was much valued even before the era of the written Bible. Egyptians, for example, took it as the stone that signified royalty for the pharaohs as well as kings. The crystal, therefore, is not just a great enhancement to beauty, but also one with religious significance and a touch of royalty.

Diamonds

The most prominent religious significance is in Hindu. From as long ago as 15 centuries, Hindus took diamonds as being protective of their owners against anything bad – ranging from evil spirits; poisonous snakes; illness; and such dangers. Then in other cultural beliefs they were believed to enhance the courage of the bearer; faithfulness; and even love.

Emeralds

You will find the emerald crystals appearing in the Bible, not just as ornaments for Cleopatra, the lady who was associated with Caesar and who ruled Egypt for a while, but you will also notice the presence of the emerald mines within the vicinity of the Red Sea. And the crystals were mined in centuries dating back to 1650BC.

And on coming to more recent years, you find the emerald stone garnishing the fourth layer of the foundation of the wall of Jerusalem; among other precious stones like topaz and sapphire.

It may also be worth mentioning that as Christian legends associated the crystal with resurrection, Romans associated it with Venus, the goddess of love; and by extension, fertility. Not surprising then, the stone is still associated with love as well as harmony.

Jasper

Jasper is one of those precious stones that lined up Aaron's breastplate as representative of one of Israel's tribes; being the twelfth. You then find it on the foundation of the wall of Jerusalem, as actually the very first precious stone to enhance the wall's beauty. It was often used to symbolized God's magnificence and glory.

Pearls

These are mentioned in the New Testament to underline the beauty of Heaven. In fact, in the era of Jesus of the Bible, pearls were the in-thing. In fact, you can see how highly the pearl was valued when you learn that Julius Caesar parted with a whopping $1 million for one singular pearl.

Rubies

You will find rubies being mentioned often in the Biblical Old Testament. Their value goes pretty high particularly because of how rare they are to find. In fact, they only surfaced within the Roman Empire around 300BC. Ruby is another mark of royalty, and even Emperor Kublai Khan of China was alleged to have offered a whole city just to get a sizeable ruby in return. (The things rulers do for self aggrandizement!)

Sapphire

This precious crystal also appears in the Holy Bible, although it is not clear if the piece they referred to as sapphire is the same sapphire of today. In the Bible, it comes across as a form of jacinth; then it is said to have traces of gold; said to have an azure color; little mix ups that make one think they may have been talking of lapis lazuli.

Topaz

This one, of course, is one of those crystals on Aaron's breastplate representing one of Israel's tribes. In fact, it came second. You then find it on the wall of Jerusalem as the ninth crystal to enhance its beauty. In the days of Europe's Middle Ages, it was worn to endear you to leaders – kings as well as civil authorities. It was even said to enhance mental abilities. And even in 18th century Spain and Egypt, the crystals marked royalty.

Chapter 6:
How Crystals Work

By now, you can probably begin to realize exactly how important it is to balance your chakras. While researchers are still studying links between the spiritual, emotional, mental, and physical realms, the chakra system is backed by thousands of years of practice. Innumerable people across decades and all parts of the world have found that taking proper care to maintain their chakras is an effective way to boost mental and physical health, and to combat serious issues.

In fact, many of the potential issues listed above that can result from imbalanced chakras seem quite frightening - you probably didn't know that diseases found in major organs could be affected by something like your energy field. Yet, it makes sense - after all, each of us is made up of energy, and the way in which our energy reacts with that of our surroundings naturally has an effect on us. Of course, sometimes this effect can be positive, but in many cases, the toxins and negative energy sources we're exposed to have a detrimental effect on us.

That's why crystals are so important. Despite efforts to eat clean, reduce your carbon footprint, or exercise regularly, your chakras still need an extra boost to be perfectly regulated. Healing crystals hold the key to unlocking unlimited wellness potential within your mind and body.

It seems crazy, probably, to anyone who isn't familiar with the concept. How could a rock possibly have any sort of healing processes? We'll explain.

As we mentioned above, the most important aspect of balancing your chakras is ensuring the fact that their vibratory frequencies are resonating at their ideal levels. An irregularity can occur from a disturbance, which causes the vibratory pattern to be thrown off. Consequently, we feel out of sorts, either in a mental or physical capacity, or both. Healing crystals, then, have the capacity to regulate these patterns and restore harmony within our chakras.

To explain it simply, crystals, like all other aspects of our world, have their own distinct vibratory patterns. Yet, healing crystals emit some of the purest resonances, thanks to their innate, balanced structure. The vibrations they offer our chakras act as tuning forks, bringing our energy field back to the level at which it vibrates most efficiently, thereby restoring health and harmony. Yet, you must allow yourself to be mentally, physically, and spiritually receptive to these restorations, which can be an issue for some nonbelievers.

To anyone who discredits the value of healing crystals, it's important to understand that there is, in fact, a scientific facet to this practice. Think of it this way: it's a known fact that despite the classifications of gasses, liquids, and solids, nothing is every truly wholly "solid;" rather, anything that's solid is made up of a series of moving atoms, in addition to molecules and minerals. Thus, the atoms that are moving among us have energy about them.

People, therefore, are complex beings, made up of energy fields that embody nature's balance and organizational properties. Just as our chakra patterns are unique, so, too, is each crystal's. The pattern at which each stone resonates corresponds best with specific chakras. To heal ourselves holistically, we can choose certain crystals to best harmonize the chakras among us that may have experienced an imbalance. Each crystal is an active participant in nature with a valuable purpose. In the next chapter, we'll offer step-by-step instructions on how to use crystals to heal yourself.

Chapter 7:
Can Crystals Heal the Psychic Way?

If the question relates to healing from a spiritual perspective; that healing that goes beyond the physical realm and touches on your mind and soul, then yes – crystals can do that. In any case, are you ever able to visually see the energy flow within the crystals? Can you even measure that energy in terms of kilojoules... no – kilowatts... no – whatever... even using Vogel's Omega 5 thing; as it links up with your bodily energies? Surely not like your conventional measuring.

But you know that the crystals are rich in natural energy and you are a product of nature as a human being, and so the energy in the crystals can traverse your physical being and reach the planes that give you a higher understanding of yourself and better perception of the world you live in.

What crystals are good for psychic healing?

Just as in matters physical, you cannot go using every crystal for random needs and expect effective solutions. Of course, you may feel like things are going well as most natural crystals usually have a positive impact on your being, but you cannot really get the satisfaction you need unless you use those crystals with relevant energies.

Different Crystals and their part in enhancing your psychic abilities

Azurite

This copper carbonate mineral has vibrations that enhance the workings of your third eye. And when you hear improving the state of your third eye, it comes with elevated levels of intuition and a high spiritual connection. As you are aware, your third eye resides where your brow chakra is; on your forehead. The energy flow from this azurite crystal connects from the third eye to your throat chakra, hence enhancing psychic communication. So you see? With heightened awareness and effective communication, how can you not straighten things out at a spiritual level?

Bloodstone

This crystal has strong energies whose frequency of vibrations matches that of your root chakra. In addition to elevating your intuition level, the crystal also has the effect of having you emotionally grounded; feeling well protected. It helps to unblock any part that is a hindrance to the flow of energy within your subtle body. And with your spiritual energies flowing unmarred, you are better placed for divine connection.

Carnelian

This crystal gives you a good balance between your root and your sacral chakra. And you know while the root chakra has to do with things physical, the sacral chakra has to do with things sensual. Anyway, the best part of how this crystal works is that it makes you trust your intuition, thus enabling you to explore your spiritual plane with relative ease. In fact, if you are into clairvoyance and clairaudience, the carnelian crystal should be your regular crystal. It will give you psychic protection; help you explore your psychic abilities; and make transitioning from the worldly to the spiritual realm and the reverse a matter-of-fact kind of thing.

Emerald

This crystal that primarily matches the heart chakra, helps bring about a much needed balance between your upper and lower chakras. In addition, it enhances your intuition and psychic protection. With your emerald consistently with you, seeing into the future becomes easy. And, of course, you do not get those fears that make you hesitate delving deeper into your spiritual zone.

Herkimer Diamond

This clear crystal even enhances the power of other crystals around it. In general it enhances energy all round your body and strengthens your psychic abilities. It sharpens your telepathy and clairvoyance, and helps you connect with your spiritual guides. It is one crystal that enables you to see your past life with more clarity, something that can help you streamline your current life and chart a great way into the future.

Kyanite

In addition to this crystal giving you psychic protection, it also has the ability to heal your chakras and balance your auras. You can also bank on it to sharpen your telepathy; lucid dreaming; and your abilities in astral travel. In general, this is a crystal that enhances your intuition and all your psychic abilities.

Lapis Lazuli

This is a great crystal when it comes to aiding connection between you and your spirit guides; and with the angels as well. Due to its strength, you need to be careful how you handle it. Of course, it is great for protecting you from psychic attacks especially if you are opening up during a psychic reading. It connects well with your throat chakra, and thus enhances your psychic communication. And on the overall, you have this chakra enhancing your psychic abilities and increasing your clairvoyance.

Moonstone

This crystal that also goes by the reference, psychic gemstone, is a must-have if you are into the use of divination tools, say, tarot cards; crystal balls; rune stones; pendulums; and such. It heightens your spiritual awareness and helps you communicate with your spiritual guides.

Snowflake Obsidian

This is the crystal that you need as you prepare for meditation. It calms your mind and then enhances your clairaudience. It can help you channel spirits appropriately and also block psychic attacks. You can be sure it will enhance your psychic abilities as a whole and you can even use it as your scrying tool when you want to get to higher spiritual realms.

Sugilite

This crystal protects you from any negative energy that can be a health risk. It helps you in channeling and in your automatic writing. It enhances the workings of your third eye as well as other chakras, making you more self aware. It helps you also to remain grounded. This is the crystal they call the healer's stone.

Amethyst

This crystal is very handy when it comes to enhancing your psychic abilities. Not only does it help you during meditation, it also boosts your level of clairvoyance; clairaudience; and also telepathy. It works well with both the crown as well as your heart chakras. If you are into psychic reading, this is the best crystal to have in preparation.

Calcite

In matters psychic, the calcite crystal is the one you need when you are into astral travel; channeling; and other out of body experiences. Of course, these are experiences that culminate in ridding your body of any unwanted spiritual forces, leaving you with a healthy mind and more intuitive mind.

Chrysocolla

This crystal is great at re-energizing your chakras. And, of course, with enhanced energy flow you get a better body balance and your health is enhanced. If you would like to elevate your spiritual awareness to the dream state, this crystal is great for you.

Fluorite

The fluorite crystal is great in cleansing your auras. It is also great in protection against intense negative energies. Needless to say, keeping negative vibrations at bay is one way of ensuring you are not prone to ill health. And if you are looking forward to serious meditation or you are preparing for a session of psychic reading, the fluorite crystal is a great one to have around.

Iolite

The iolite crystal enhances your self-awareness and heightens your intuition to the level of having vivid psychic visions. With this crystal, you can accomplish a lot as far as physical and spiritual healing goes because it has the brand of energy needed by mediums; tarot readers; astrologers; and such other people who usually get in touch with their higher planes.

Labradolite

This crystal that also goes by the reference Wizard Stone has powerful energies that link you up with your spirit guides. It also protects you from negative psychic forces especially when you have opened up during psychic reading sessions.

Malachite

You can use this crystal to cleanse your auras and also to balance your energy chakras. As you know, imbalances in your chakras make you feel unwell. This crystal that also goes by the reference Peacock Stone increases your rate of healthy dreaming. It also enhances your visions especially when you use it together with the azurite crystal. And basically, the malachite crystal works in league with the heart chakra.

Quartz

The quartz, which is also referred to as the Universal Crystal, mainly works in league with the Crown chakra, enhancing as well as expanding your psychic abilities. It is also able to balance your chakras so that you end up having a great sense of well being. With this crystal, your abilities in clairvoyance and also psychic visions are enhanced, and you are able to comprehend spiritual messages in a better way.

Sapphire

This crystal has such effective energy that it enhances your ability to communicate with the spiritual world. You can particularly witness your level of telepathy going up; your out of body experiences getting easier; and everything to do with your third eye improving.

Turquoise

The turquoise is a great health boost as it activates your energy centers, clearing blocked chakras and making communication with higher realms relatively easy. It enhances your spiritual awareness, improving your clairaudience as well as your clairvoyance. In all this, the crystal works with your brow as well as throat chakra. And as long as you have the turquoise crystal, your health will not be jeopardized by negative energies.

Now you can clearly see that it is possible to use crystals for your psychic healing; being a partnership of two processes that are individually effective but even more effective when working together. What makes this mode of healing even more convenient is the fact that you have individual crystals matching specific chakras in your body, which means you can effectively address specific issues of ill health faster and more effectively.

Chapter 8: Acquiring Your Crystals

There are many different crystals that serve specific purposes when it comes to balancing our energy fields. While some individuals choose to keep a variety of crystals on hand or within their living spaces, it's best to first develop an understanding about how you can use crystals to target certain chakras, so that you can incorporate them to heal any mental or physical maladies you may be experiencing.

First, however, you must learn how to effectively use the stone so that you can reap the benefits of its healing properties.

To begin with, you'll need to select your crystal or gemstone. Keep in mind the purpose for which you are using the crystal healing method. Whether it's to alleviate headaches, tension, or simply realign your chakras, focus on one specific goal when you are beginning your selection process.

Although it's not necessary for you to have a full understanding of each crystal and its designated healing purpose, it can be helpful to have some knowledge of what types of crystals you should look for when making your purchase. For a full guide as to which crystals help specific issues and work best to realign each chakra, take a look at chapter five.

Some crystal healing specialists recommend using the "first sight" method to choose crystals or gems. If you are visiting a store or looking online to purchase crystals, you may find one that simply catches your eye. For some inexplicable reason, you feel drawn to that crystal or gemstone, and you continue to focus your attention on it. More likely than not, that stone or gem is intended for your use, and it will be beneficial to your practice. Even if you feel some doubt or do not have a full understanding as to how the crystal could benefit you, it's in your best interest to purchase it and use it in your practice. Intuition is a very powerful tool in the crystal healing practice, so it will behoove you to listen to yours as you seek out your crystal or gemstone.

Another means for acquiring the proper crystal for your practice is to use the vibration test. If you have access to a store or merchant that supplies crystals, place your hand on it to see if you can sense any kind of vibration. If you feel unsure about this method, you can brush up on your sensitivity by practicing with a large piece of clear quartz crystal. Quartz is known for its versatility; sometimes, it gives off steady energy with regular pulses. Other times, people have noted that quartz crystals can feel either very warm or very cool in their hands. Quartz can even create a tingling sensation. You'll know when it feels right, even if you are unable to describe the sensation you experience from a crystal. Feel free to experiment with lots of different types of crystals in order to get a sense for the sensation that works best for you.

Sometimes, experienced crystal seekers will use a pendulum to determine whether or not a crystal or gem will benefit them. Pendulum dowsing is a supernatural practice by which individuals acquire answers to questions that might seem otherwise impossible to answer. If you are experienced with pendulum dowsing, feel free to use this technique to acquire your crystal. Go about your normal dowsing routine in and simply ask the pendulum whether or not the crystal you have in mind (remember to specify the type of the crystal) will be beneficial to you. Wait for an answer as usual. Or, pass the pendulum above the crystal or gem and observe any circular motion that it creates when it normally wouldn't. If you're inexperienced with pendulum dowsing, it may be best for you to use a different approach for acquiring your crystal or gem, as the art of dowsing is a practice that is generally acquired over time.

It may happen that at one point or another, you will be given a crystal or a gem as a gift. Instead of stowing it away, use this opportunity to your advantage. It could be that you were in need of this crystal, but just didn't know it. In a sense, the crystal or gem has "found" you, and it can be used to your benefit. Likewise, keep in mind that if you lose one of your favorite crystals, its purpose in your life may have been fulfilled. More likely than not, it has gone on to serve a new purpose elsewhere.

Sometimes, especially for beginners, there is only a select variety of crystals that one can choose among. Perhaps you don't have access to a store or merchant that sells a wide variety of crystals, or you've been given one as a gift to start your practice. Even if you don't feel an immediate connection with the select crystal you've acquired, it is possible that you will, in time, establish a bond with it. Thus, it's important not to rule out any crystal that doesn't immediately feel right to you. It's very likely that with enough time, the crystal or gem will become of great use to you. The crystal or gem can become tuned into your vibration, meaning that it will be very rewarding for you to use in your practice.

If your only option right now is to purchase a crystal via the internet, you'll need to rely more heavily on your intuition when making your decision. Take your time looking through images of various crystals, and take note of the ones that you feel drawn towards. If you notice the sensation of wanting to reach out and touch a crystal, it's likely that the particular crystal you're looking at will align with your goals. You may even feel such an overwhelming desire to acquire the crystal that you'll become frustrated with the fact that you cannot, at the present moment, reach out and touch it. Pay close attention to any crystal or gem that makes you feel that way - it's a strong indication that you must acquire it for your practice, and that it will hold significant value in your life.

Nonetheless, there's a chance that you won't feel any sort of pull towards a crystal, regardless of the method you're using to acquire it. Resist the urge to purchase a crystal or gem simply for the sake of having it. If there is absolutely no connection between you and your tool, it isn't going to benefit you in your practice. It could just be that you're having an "off" day, and that you'll need to return to the store, website, or place in which you're trying to acquire a crystal at a later time. There's no shame in simply not being drawn to any crystals at all. It simply means that the timing isn't right. Patience is an important tool in the practice of crystal healing. Knowing when to wait is one factor that can separate a good practice from one that is truly great.

At the same time, you must also remain open to all kinds of possibilities when seeking out a crystal. It could be that you go into a shop or visit a website with the intention of purchasing one specific type of crystal to fulfill your needs, but you're somehow drawn towards a different type of crystal or gem entirely. Trust your unconscious and abandon your previous thoughts about the type of crystal or gem that you "should" buy; recognize instead that your higher level of self has skipped right over any additional steps and has identified the single crystal that will most appropriately fit with your practice. In fact, realize that if this phenomenon happens to you, you're actually quite lucky.

Chapter 9:
Are Crystals Suitable for Kids?

Do you think some parents may be concerned about their kids handling crystals? Maybe that is a possibility. Considering that some people still view crystals as items of mystery, it is understandable that some may still hesitate to let their children handle them. However, after going through such an enlightening text as this book, such tension is likely to melt away and give way to appreciation of the positive way in which crystals impact your life.

Left alone, do you think children would go for crystals? Of course, they would! The attraction towards crystals is actually natural, not just because glowing beauty is bound to attract anyone, but also the energy the crystals possess has a way of relating to that of children. You need to remember that every person has that spiritual energy flowing within them. However, when it comes to kids and their innocence, you can visualize how pure that energy is, and how smooth it flows. How compatible it is then with that of the pure natural crystals!

Introducing Crystals to Children

If you are making a conscious effort to introduce crystals to kids, it is best to begin with those that you are certain are physically suitable.

Begin with tumbled crystals

These ones are smooth on the surface and so you can be sure they would not occasion injury to the young ones. They are also easy on the hand as they are relatively light. And, of course, you need not worry about breakage as those ones that you give them are not fragile.

Allow the kids to make their choice

After ensuring that the crystals around do not have rough edges and are not fragile, you can let the kids explore and make their pick. The kid will pick this one, leave it; pick another one, return it; until ultimately the child remains with the crystal that suits his or her personally. By allowing such an environment, you are letting the natural processes of energy flow and compatibility with colors and shapes work uninhibited. That obviously leaves the kid with the crystal that is naturally helpful to him or her, and not with just a specimen of beauty.

Parents are understandably very sensitive when it comes to their kids. You wonder whether this or that other crystal might elicit too much energy and excitement; or too much calm in your kid for comfort. An informed guideline would, thus, be very handy.

Here is a great guide on what crystals are best for your kids:

Amethyst

This is one of those crystals that you can insert in a pouch and then place nicely under the pillow of your child's bed. And why is it deemed great for kids? First of all, something that will enhance a good night's sleep is always welcome when it comes to young ones – they need long hours of blissful sleep, says the doctor (yours and mine). And that is what amethyst does with its calming effect to the mind and ability to reduce stress.

Remember even for you, the adult, it brings you a sense of contentment; stability; and overall inner peace. In fact, when you hear of the crystal that embodies both spirituality as well as contentment, look no further; amethyst is it. And do not underscore how visual kids are. In the case of amethyst, its purple color is irresistible to kids.

Agate

Do you think kids could ever have enough of colored stuff? No way! And that tells you automatically that they would be attracted to crystals that are multi-colored the way agate is. You can find almost any color in agate crystals.

The crystal is generally associated with courage as well as strength; and when it comes to your kids, it is going to stabilize their emotions – barring fears and anxieties. In the same vein it contributes to your child gaining self confidence. And, on the overall, you will be glad to know that it has the effect of clearing negative energies.

Clear Quartz

If you recall, in helpful processes like in meditation, you want to have a clear mind. Now, this is what your kids get too when they hold onto clear quartz crystals. They become more self aware and their thinking is clear and well defined. With no dull blockages in the flow of energy, the clear quartz has the effect of amplifying your kid's energy and enhancing its flow; thus clearing away any negative vibe.

Rose Quartz

The rose quartz comes in pink; and beautiful pink at that. This crystal transmits plenty of loving energy. And you want that for your kid – being able to love unconditionally; being easy in forgiving; being compassionate; and being able to express their emotions. With this strong effect from the rose quartz, your child enjoys innermost healing and a sense of self worth. As a result the kid is able to settle in healthy relationships marked by harmony.

Green Aventurine

If you want a crystal that guides your child to know that the world does not come to a halt just because something has gone amiss, the green aventurine is it. It is a crystal that gives your kid emotional peace and a positive outlook to life. On top of that it stimulates the mind, bringing out creativity and enhancing motivation. It not only gives your kid a sense of joy but also one of independence. And the good thing is that this crystal also has a balancing act because, at the same time, it elicits compassion as well as empathy in the kid. It even makes the kid slow to anger, something that is great for relationships.

Carnelian

This one has very attractive colors for kids – from orange all the way to very dark red. And it is one of those that stimulate the kid's creativity. It evokes some warm energy that makes the kid very perceptive to what is happening in his or her life.

Tiger Eye

This one too has colors that attract children's attention – yellow and also brown. It has the effect of making the kid grounded by enhancing courage and self confidence. It also makes the kid feel lucky and well protected. This crystal is another one that enhances the kid's perception and improves his or her ability to make sound decisions. It is safe to say that the Tiger Eye crystal enhances a kid's intuition.

And do children really understand how crystals work?

Good question, but really, do they need to? Is their knowledge or lack of it of any consequence? How much do kids understand about other good things, like say, a balanced diet? Little or nothing... But does that prevent the benefits from flowing? Not at all – kids may eat bacon because it is delicious but the parents know they served it for the protein. In the same way, kids may love the crystals for their sharp colors; their shape; their texture; or even their radiance, but at the end of the day, it is the natural energy flow that will benefit them even in their innocent ignorance.

How safe are crystals with kids?

Parents can sometimes over-react. Just because you are aware that some crystal is precious or valuable is no reason to make you paranoid about your kid losing it. Do you refrain from dressing your kid in expensive cashmere in winter just because he or she is not under your care all day long? How about beautiful and valuable earrings? No, you do not. Rather, you dress your kid as you deem fit as a matter-of-fact. That is exactly how you need to handle crystals.

- You can fit them on a pendant and let them wear it the way they would a necklace

- You can help them wear it as part of normal jewelry

- You can put it nicely in a pouch which you then ask them to carry in their pocket the way they carry personal effects like handkerchiefs

- You can have your kid carry the crystal in a special box

As time goes by, your kid is going to understand the underlying value of crystals and may even suggest to you when it is time to have a different category of crystal. In the meantime, it may suffice to have your kid carry the crystal as a personal item for bringing good luck.

Chapter 10:
Crystal Healing and Pregnant Mothers

The great thing about crystals is that whatever crystal is safe on normal days is also safe during pregnancy. Nothing about crystals poses extra danger to a pregnant woman. In fact, a good number of crystals are actually helpful during this time of hormonal imbalance, anxiety and mood swings. So unless you have extraneous issues accompanying your pregnancy, crystal therapy should be just fine for you.

What makes pregnant women require crystal therapy even more?

For one all senses are much more improved when one is pregnant, and the level of intuition is extra heighted. In fact, a pregnant mother feels a stronger connection with her whole being – her own body, mind and soul, plus the life of the baby growing in her. For that reason, crystals are very important in moderating all the senses and bringing calmness in the expectant mother. Crystals come very handy all the journey through; from conception, through pregnancy, during birth, and even during postnatal recuperation.

Crystals that are greatly recommended for pregnant mothers

The moonstone stands tall in all this. Not only does it bring the expectant mother harmony, it also brings her good fortune. And when it comes to harmony, it is not just harmony within the person herself but also harmony between her and the people around her.

How, exactly, does the moonstone help?

This crystal of love, mainly associated with the crown chakra as well as the third eye, has unique healing benefits for an expectant mother. They include:

- Improving the digestive system

- Improving the state of the entire reproductive system

- Enhancement of the process of toxin elimination from the body

- Dealing with the problem of fluid retention

- Improving the health of the pregnant mother's skin

- Improving the health of the expectant mother's hair

- Giving the expectant mother a great complexion

- Helps to enhance contractions during labor

- It is said to enhance healthy lactation

One thing you need to know is that the benefits of using the moonstone do not begin with pregnancy. The crystal is also beneficial before pregnancy, especially for someone trying to improve her fertility. This means you have higher chances of conceiving when using the moonstone crystal than otherwise. And even as a nursing mother, the benefits of using the moonstone are still evident.

Other crystals that are also beneficial during pregnancy

The amazonite

This crystal that is famed for rejuvenating both the heart and the throat chakras saves a pregnant woman from muscle cramps. As you may know, these cramps are usually in form of leg cramps, although at times they may affect the feet. They often affect the lower part of the leg during the 2nd and 3rd trimesters. Every expectant mother will get excited at having some non-medical therapy to get rid of this unpleasant, and sometimes painful, experience.

Aventurine

This crystal that is associated with the heart chakra is a healer when it comes to morning sickness; heartburn; as well as indigestion – a combination of complications associated with pregnancy.

Carnelian

Are you aware that labor time is a period of anxiety? With all the anticipation and pain; uncertainty and fears; an expectant woman could well do with some calming down. That is what the carnelian, a crystal closely linked to the base chakra, does. It calms down the woman in labor and also quells her anxiety. This is understandable considering that the base chakra is located in the neighborhood of the pelvic floor; an area very much affected by labor pains and associated discomforts.

Citrine

This crystal that is associated with the solar plexus helps to solve the problem of constipation in pregnant mothers.

Hematite

Hematite, a crystal associated with the root or base chakra, helps to get rid of muscle cramps in expectant mothers, the same way the amazonite does.

The labradorite

This crystal that is associated with the crown chakra helps to solve the problem of elevated blood pressure, a common problem with expectant mothers.

Lapis lazuli

This crystal that works well together with both the throat as well as the brow chakra is also helpful in lowering blood pressure in expectant mothers. It is also helpful in stabilizing the woman's mood. In fact, the use of lapis lazuli is very ancient as in the 17th century it was still used on expectant mothers who had a history of difficult deliveries. In that era, the lapis crystals were crushed and then made into medicinal syrup by the name of Alkermes Syrup.

The Rose quartz

This great healing crystal that is associated with the heart chakra does a good job of reducing swellings that sometimes dominate the period of a woman's pregnancy. It is also great at curing the hypertension that sometimes develops during pregnancy.

The turquoise

The turquoise, a crystal associated with the throat chakra, is very handy in reducing the prevalence of Braxton Hicks contractions, thus protecting the baby in the woman's womb.

The amethyst

The amethyst crystals, which are directly linked to the third eye, are great in enhancing the welfare of an expectant mother. Not only do they give the woman a divine connection, they also help to stabilize her emotions while at the same time alleviating any emotional pain she may be suffering. They also relieve her of physical tension as well as physical pain.

Black onyx

This crystal that is associated with the root chakra is very helpful during childbirth. It is known to accelerate the healing of the mother's wound and also protect her from any affliction. It also enhances her strength as well as stamina at childbirth.

In fact, traditionally, some cultures are known to have given expectant mothers bags containing onyx crystals to hold onto when in labor, as an effort to get pain relief and also speed up the process of delivery.

The bloodstone

If there is one crystal that is great at rejuvenation, it is the bloodstone. It gives the woman strength after she has lost a lot of it during labor, and it also hastens the healing process. It actually does wonders for a tired mind and exhausted body and is good for pain relief. Therapists believe the bloodstone crystal is capable of stopping a potential miscarriage.

Carnelian

This crystal that works well with both the root as well as the sacral chakras is a good one to wear throughout a woman's pregnancy. It keeps away negative emotions, including fear and anxiety during pregnancy and even at childbirth. The carnelian is also great at keeping the expectant mother motivated and energetic; and also courageous and with healthy levels of self esteem.

Chrysocolla

This crystal that is directly linked to the throat chakra clears from the mind of the pregnant mother any fear based thoughts. It actually brings much needed tranquility to the mind as well as the heart of the woman. As such the expectant woman is able to handle her changing situation with a positive mind free of mental tension. This crystal is also said to reduce labor related pain as well as ease the process of childbirth.

Larimar

This crystal that is associated with the throat chakra brings serenity and tranquility into the life of an expectant mother. It is known for soothing edgy nerves as well as reducing stress and anxiety. It also has unique ability to re-tune the woman's natural femininity, restoring her connection with nature. Larimar comes in handy even after the woman has given birth as it is capable of clearing post partum depression.

Malachite

This crystal that is actually dedicated to the heart chakra is very precious to expectant mothers. Not only does it stabilize their emotions and get rid of the negative impact of past traumas, it also eases the pains of childbirth and enhances safety at the time of delivery. The crystal is also great at stimulating contractions during labor. This crystal is so helpful at childbirth that it has been nicknamed, *Midwives' Stone*.

Moss agate

This crystal that is associated with heart chakra is seen as a crystal of new beginnings. This is apt for an expectant mother who keeps anticipating the birth of her new baby. The crystal clears any fears the expectant woman may have had and fills her with hope as well as optimism. At the same time, the moss agate increases the level of the woman's self esteem as well as self confidence. You can also use this crystal to reduce the intensity of pain at childbirth.

Orange calcite

This crystal that is linked to both the root as well as the sacral chakras is valued in the case of a pregnant woman because it clears building fears as well as tension; and generally wipes away stress by getting the expectant mother in the mode of positive thinking. The crystal is also credited with the capability of healing the woman's reproductive system.

The Peridot

This crystal that is associated with the heart chakra is credited with the capability of stimulating contractions, and also enhancing the opening of the birth canal to make the delivery experience relatively easy for the mother. It is also credited with keeping postpartum depression at bay. Peridot's energy helps to clear apathy as well as exhaustion, thus saving the expectant mother from lethargy and hopelessness. By using the peridot crystal, all feelings of guilt, obsession and other negative feelings disappear; and you have the expectant mother becoming more self aware.

Picture Jasper

This crystal that is linked to the base chakra is said to clear any fears the expectant mother may have, and also reduce pain during delivery.

Even with this wealth of knowledge about the role different crystals play in enhancing the wellbeing of an expectant mother, it is always important for the mother to feel the crystal resonating with her purpose. After all, the energies from the crystals and those from the mother will be linking up and settling on energy vibrations suitable for the mother and her unborn baby.

Chapter 11:
Preparing Your Crystals or Gems

Once you obtain your crystal, either as a gift or by purchasing it, you may want to clear it. If a crystal feels "off" - for example, if it seems as if it's too heavy or gives you a feeling of negativity when you hold it -then it most likely needs to be cleared. While it's not necessarily a bad thing if a crystal has already received another individual's imprint, made up of thoughts, emotions, and unique energy, your practice will be most beneficial if you clear a crystal and make it truly your own. You can do this by removing the stored vibrations, or "clearing" it. Crystals that are ready and have been cleared will emanate positivity and will feel tingly and cold to the touch.

You can use a variety of methods to clear your crystals. For one, you may wish to use the "smudging" method, in which you pass the crystal through the smoke of a burning sage or cedar stick. Originally adapted by Native Americans, this is one of the most popular methods for clearing gems and crystals. You can acquire cedar or sage at many specialty stores or herbal shops. This method is most advantageous for clearing any jewelry you may have with gems or crystals in it.

Experienced crystal healers sometimes choose to use the sea salt method to clear crystals. If you are a beginner, you may find that this method is a bit harsh. However, if you are experienced with crystal and gem healing and are looking for a different way to clear your crystals, you may want to give this a try. Simply fill a glass or ceramic container with sea salt and bury your crystal in it overnight. Or, use a combined mixture of water and sea salt and plunge your crystal or gem in it for the duration of one to three days. If you choose this method, follow your intuition to determine how much salinity you should use, and the amount of time for which you should keep the crystal submerged. Make sure that you rinse your crystal completely before using it to eliminate any salt, preferably with filtered water.

Another means of clearing a crystal or gem is to use your breath. If your crystal is small enough to fit into one hand, place it in your dominant hand. If not, hold it with both hands. While doing so, focus your intention on the crystal and actively think about freeing all negativity from it. As you maintain this thought, inhale through your nose. As you exhale, breathe forcefully out through your mouth. The breath acts as a means of clearing the crystal.

You can also clear them by placing them outside at night from the full moon to the new moon phases. You may also bury your crystal in dried herbs, such as myrrh or sandalwood, or even into the earth. It's recommended that crystals are cleared after each healing exercise, as they must have their frequencies restored. Again, your intuition is the most powerful tool that you can use to determine how and when a crystal or gem must be cleared. If you can sense that the crystal is no longer as powerful as it once was, or you can visibly see cloudiness, you should perform a clearing. You should also clear your crystal or gem if it ever feels sticky to the touch.

It's also a good idea to dedicate your healing crystal before use. As your goal will be to use the crystal for healing purposes, you can choose to dedicate it to a healing goddess, such as Isis or Yemaya. To dedicate the stone, you simply must hold the crystal in your hand and focus its intent on healing purposes.

Another step many crystal healers take before beginning their practice is charging the gem or crystal. Another term for charging your crystal is revitalizing it. To do this, you must first establish the type of energy that you're seeking. There are specific places and times for placing crystals to charge them that work well with corresponding energies, but you can use your imagination and intuition to establish what will work best. Some practitioners have found that simply burying a crystal in the snow or earth or placing it directly in moonlight, sunlight, or atop a larger crystal cluster works well.

Nonetheless, there are specific pairings that seem to work best for charging crystals and gems with specific energy intentions. Consult the list below to figure out the best time or place to charge your crystal, depending on your energy intention.

- Passion or happiness: Charge during the summer solstice.

- Rebirth or renewal: Charge during the winter solstice.

- Growth: Charge during the spring equinox.

- Harvesting of dreams: Charge during the autumnal equinox.

- Cleansing: Place crystal or gem in a clear, purifying stream.

- Vitality or energy restoration: Place crystal or gem in the ocean during high tide.

- Restfulness or relaxation: Place crystal or gem in the ocean during low tide.

- Abundance or love: Charge during full moon phase.

- Introspection: Charge during dark moon phase.

- Optimism or hope: Charge during new moon phase.

Once you have completed these steps, you are ready to perform your healing practice by using crystals or gems. There are a few different approaches you can use, some of which are more involved than others. We will discuss these methods below.

Chapter 12:
A Step-By-Step Guide to Using Crystals

You can elect to either use a passive crystal healing method or an active one. Some people choose to use a passive approach when they are just beginning their practice. This means that instead of actively performing any kind of routine, you will simply keep your crystal nearby. While the effect will not be as significant as it would be if you chose to use an active approach, you will still experience subtle differences within your energy field. For some, this is enough. You will be able to witness a slight shift within your mental energy, and everything should become a bit more balanced and harmonious than it previously was. Keep crystals around you to perpetuate these improvements.

One of the most powerful ways to use crystals or gems for healing is to use affirmations. Affirmations are thoughts or statements that lead to a certain outcome. In other words, affirmations are used as a means of helping us achieve goals or acquire the things we want. It's important to actively pay attention to your affirmations, instead of succumbing to routine statements or thoughts. Also, it can be helpful to try to rid yourself of previous affirmations that you've carried with you which may not be beneficial to your life. Those around us are responsible for influencing our affirmations, but it is important to try to develop a set of your own. Consciously recognize negative affirmations; only then will you be able to get rid of them.

Likewise, it's important to find the positivity in a negative situation. Even if there's something that's bothered you about a situation in the past, it can benefit you to try to find the good in it. Visualize positivity, and actively seek the feelings of reward that you might experience when achieving your goals.

If you've developed affirmations, you can move on to programming your crystal. This is a necessary step to attune your crystal's energetic charge with your own visualizations and thoughts. This will help your dreams to manifest in a tangible manner.

Typically, quartz crystals are used for programming, but you may also choose among other variations. If you are searching for love, you may elect to use rose quartz, whereas turquoise and aquamarine are beneficial for creativity. If your situation relates to physical health, you may use aventurine, and citrine can be used for abundance.

To program your stone, you may hold your crystal in both hands and gaze at it actively. Breathe deeply, and inhale through your nose and release through your mouth. Visualize what it is that you are trying to achieve: clearly call into your mind the specific objective that you're seeking, whether it's improved health, a new job, or a rewarding relationship. Clearly visualize it, and vocalize an affirmation as you do so. Call upon your consciousness to provide a feel for what it would be like to actually have the thing that you desire. Every time you exhale, imagine sending your desire directly into your gem or crystal. If you are able to do this successfully, you will have programmed your crystal, and its vibration will be set with the intention you provided.

You may also choose to use written affirmations. This one is perhaps one of the simplest - yet also most effective - means of using healing crystals. Whatever it is that you are searching for, write it down on a piece of paper. Then, take your crystal of choice and place it atop the note.

Some individuals choose to meditate with crystals in order to achieve healing. Even if you are unfamiliar with meditation or have never tried it before, it can be wondrously beneficial and may lead to healing, new insights, and a more positive, unobstructed outlook on your situation. While meditation does require a bit of practice, it is a skill that can eventually be learned. It may be difficult for you to learn to quiet your mind at first, but it is extremely beneficial, especially when performed with crystals.

If you exercise regularly, you may already have an advantage over non-exercisers when it comes to meditation. That's because many crystal healers believe that meditation can come easily during the actual process of exercise. To do it, simply visualize the smooth, free-flowing movement of your body and your breath. By placing complete focus on the present and the act that you're doing, you are already meditating. To enhance your practice, begin repeating affirmations to yourself as you exercise. State the affirmation at least three times, and visualize the outcome. As you go about your exercise, hold a clear quartz crystal either in one or both of your hands. If you're repeating affirmations, make sure that the pointed ends of the crystal are directed away from you. If, however, you are hoping to receive light and energy, you should instead hold the crystal with the points facing towards you.

If you are currently unable to perform exercise, do not worry. There is another, less active way in which you can meditate. Simply sit or lie down in a position that's comfortable for you. Make sure that you will not experience any disturbances, such as interruptions from family members or phone calls. Create a space in which you will be alone in silence.

Many beginners have found that meditation recordings are extremely effective for guiding them through their first few meditations. It can be overwhelming to try to figure out what one should do with his or her mind during the first meditation, but a recording can guide the mind through the proper channels. If you prefer not to use a guided meditation, you can always meditate on your own by repeating affirmations, as previously discussed. Think about the energy flowing throughout your body as you breathe, and concentrate on the act of breathing. Imagine a means by which you can extract distracting thoughts from your mind. As you continue your meditation practice, your ability to rid your mind of distracting thoughts will improve. To receive the greatest benefit of your meditation practice, hold a clear quartz crystal in one or both hands, as mentioned above.

One other, very simple way to use healing crystals is to place them underneath your pillow as you sleep at night. Many individuals find that the presence of healing crystals can help prevent sleep-related issues, such as insomnia. They are also credited for warding off nightmares. Proponents of astral projection have found that placing crystals under their pillows can assist their practice and foster out-of-body experiences. If that's something you're interested in, or if you're an experienced astral projector looking for a way to enhance your practice, consider using a crystal under your pillow at night.

Crystals can also be placed in your bathtub or on its edge as you bathe. Soak in a warm bath and relax. Not only will the bath itself soothe your body and mind, but the presence of the crystals will further refresh your spirit and physical being. If you choose to place crystals directly in the bathwater with you, then they will be able to absorb negativity, such as unpleasant emotions or energy. Rose quartz, amethyst, clear quartz and aventurine are popular choices for crystal healing used in the bathtub.

Another common crystal healing practice is called the laying of the stones. This practice rids your body of negative energy and toxins while simultaneously balancing your chakras. After you've completed this exercise, you'll find emotional release, because the vibration of your chakras will have become aligned with that of the universal grid. Your life force energy can be freed, and any disease and negativity can be transferred into health and wellness. Because the stones come into direct contact with your body and are placed near the affected chakra, the laying of the stones technique is often hailed as the most effective means of crystal healing.

You can either choose to lay the stones on your body yourself, or you may use a hands-on healing approach through the use of a practitioner (a Reiki master, for example). Place the stones along your body; aligning them with their corresponding chakras (we'll discuss this aspect in the next chapter). The crystals you choose to use can be in any form - raw, tumbled, faceted, or beads.

Once you've placed the stones, allow yourself to envision the healing properties of each stone, and repeat this process moving slowly from one chakra to the next. It's best to practice this in a quiet, calm environment. Try to "let go," and allow yourself to be drawn to the energies of each crystal. If you find yourself focusing on one crystal's energy more so than the others, this may be a good thing - it could be that the corresponding chakra was particularly imbalanced, and you're now taking the time to right it.

As you are visualizing the crystals, picture each as a bright source of energy that is harmonious and healthy, and allow it to enter your chakra. Once you are ready to move onto the next chakra, flick your fingers so as to release any negative energy that has been removed by the crystal. After you've completed this process with each chakra, it's a good idea to perform an aura brush. To do this, move the palms of both of your hands over your entire body, working your way down from your head to your toes. Do this process slowly and with intention, and take deep breaths as you do so.

Of course, you can always choose to simply place your crystals in areas of your work or living spaces. Because of environmental stressors, our bodies are exposed to higher levels of pollution than ever before. Electronic devices, plastics, and even radio waves are surrounding us on a daily basis, which has the potential to affect our chakras in a negative way. To combat this effect, you can place crystals or gems in the spaces you frequent to amplify your own personal energy fields. The enhanced vibrations will help to ward of the effects of any environmental stressors that are present. Specifically, you may want to place crystals or gems in areas where you are exposed to nylon carpets, computers, artificial lighting, metal furniture, and air conditioning. These factors are all known stressors that can be detrimental to the energy field, so placing crystals in areas that have these items can help offset the negative effects.

Chapter 13:
Reiki Healing With Crystals

Do you know what Reiki is? Definitely, there are those who may see it as a foreign looking term that has nothing to do with them while others may think it is a term associated with some oblique religion. Well, Reiki as a term has a foreign touch alright, but it is in no way oblique or a form of religion. In fact, once you understand it, you will realize it is close to the topic discussed in this book – that of minding your welfare the natural way.

The term, Reiki, is derived from the Japanese language, where *Rei* is literally a ghost and *ki,* vapor. However, when the term *Reiki* was assimilated into English, it was given the meaning befitting the context in which it was used. To be clear, that context is one of spiritual healing.

Understanding *Rei*

In this regard, then, *Rei* represents higher intelligence that actually facilitates creation and also proper functioning of the entire universe. What that means is that *Rei* influences all things, living as well as non-living. You can actually visualize it as subtle wisdom permeating all things that exist in the universe.

When it comes to human beings, it is *Rei* that they turn to for guidance when they are in need. This intelligence or wisdom is taken to be infinite and also all-knowing, to the extent that some cultures refer to it as God.

Understanding *ki*

Ki is spiritual energy – you cannot actually see it or touch it. It is actually the one that animates the things in the universe that are living. So you will find *ki* in human beings; in animals; as well as in plants. For better comprehension, just know that *ki* is equated to the well known *chi* of China; Indian *prana*; and Hawaiian *ti* or even *ki*. Other terms people use in reference to this same *ki* from Reiki include the odic force; orgone; bioplasma and even the life force.

Anyway, this energy is so central to your daily life that when its level falls you feel weak and often sickly whereas when its level is high you love life – feeling strong and confident. Can you do something about your level of *ki*? Oh yes – it is important to know that you actually acquire this energy from foods that you consume; air that you breathe; the sunshine you are exposed to; and also your sleep. Breathing exercises as well as meditation also help to boost this energy.

It is thus safe to summarize Reiki as spiritual energy whose direction is dictated or guided by higher intelligence. This practice has even been acknowledged in the field of modern medicine to have a great impact in reduction of physical pain; reduction of swelling; calming of the nervous system; and also reducing after-surgery recovery time.

Using crystals in Reiki healing

Here you are, obviously, looking at two energy sources. So this form of healing entails two energy forms boosting each other and making the healing process faster and more effective.

The stone laying step

While practicing Reiki, you usually have someone assisting you – the healer. And this healer needs to meet certain standards:

- Be supportive

- Be comforting

- Be non-judgmental

And the reason these qualities are fundamental is because the whole essence of having stones laid on you is for you to be able to let go of any spiritual blocks that could be hindering your well being; whether those be emotional or mental; or of an ethereal nature. So you need to work with someone who makes you feel safe to speak out and release your emotions.

Balancing your chakra energies using crystals

Dealing with one part of your body

What you need to do is to identify that part of your body that feels weak; that one that needs healing. Once you have identified your need, select the appropriate crystal and place it on that area. If your weakness cannot be linked directly to any part of your physical body, consider the chakra whose energies normally solve that problem. You can then proceed to place the corresponding crystal at the position of that chakra. Crystals have a way of boosting the chakra vibrations without destabilizing its energies. The impact of crystals on chakras in Reiki healing is to bring harmony to your system as a whole.

Dealing with your body in general

You may not have a distinct part of your body that you want to treat using Reiki, but you may feel like you need some energy and motivation injected into you. In such a case, you can decide to have an array of crystals each with a different role. Remember different crystals have different auras and each takes different dimensions in healing. You may, for instance, feel bad because you lack in self confidence and there is a set of crystals to deal with that. Your tummy may be bloated and there is a set of crystals for that kind of problem too. Likewise, of the seven major chakras, you can identify the one that deals with any one of those problems. In our case, therefore, you need to pick the crystal that corresponds to the problem and then place it at the position of the corresponding chakra.

- Begin by placing a grounding crystal right between your feet. Smoky quartz is a good example of such a crystal that can act as your anchor.

- Then place one crystal after the other, from bottom upwards. What you are essentially doing is toning your body as a whole, a process that leaves you feeling well and energized.

- When you deem your Reiki session over, remove your crystals, this time beginning from your upper body downwards.

How to match crystal colors with corresponding chakras

As you have already seen from the chapter on the seven chakras, each one of the chakras has a role to play in your health as well as a corresponding color. Of course the aura color may be a little shady or faded if you are not at your best, but there is the actual color that you use as a benchmark.

Red crystals

These are the ones that match your first chakra – your root chakra. They are the ones you go for when you want to boost your energy; your courage; passion; and even love. Generally, if ever you are feeling low on energy and somewhat listless, this is the color of crystal you look out for. Even when you feel emotionally low or when you realize you are having a weakness of second guessing yourself, a red colored crystal will come in handy.

Among the red crystals are red coral; the bloodstone; the garnet; red jasper; the ruby; red calcite; vanadinite; eudialyte; and even cinnabar. And considering that black and brown colored crystals are also helpful to your root chakra to some degree, you may also wish to use Onyx, obsidian, jet or even the black tourmaline.

The best body location to place the red crystal that you select is the lower end of your spine. Alternatively, you could pick two pieces of red crystal – of the same type, of course – and then place each of them at the top end of each of your legs.

Orange crystals

Orange, the color of power that also enhances your friendships and family relationships, corresponds to the sacral chakra. In comparison, whereas red is explosive, orange is thoughtful and controlled. Orange colored crystals are very helpful when you are feeling stressed out or when you are in shock – they do help to balance your emotions.

These ones include orange calcite; the carnelian; stilbite; sunstone; sardonyx; hessonite garnet; vanadinite; orange-yellow heliodor; citrine; moonstone; and also the agate.

As for the position you place the crystal that you choose, it has to be on the lower part of your abdomen, the location of your sacral chakra.

Yellow crystals

These ones correspond to the third chakra, otherwise referred to as the solar plexus. They bring you much needed optimism; warmth as well as clarity. When you are feeling nervous; exhausted; or even at the verge of burnout; yellow crystals are great to use as they protect you effectively from lethargy and even depression.

Among the crystals in this category is amber; citrine; jasper; imperial topaz; golden topaz; sunstone; lemon quartz; honey calcite; yellow fluorite; yellow calcite; and even sulphur.

The best location for your chosen yellow crystal is somewhere between your ribcage and the navel.

Green crystals

These ones correspond to the fourth chakra – the heart chakra. This is actually the color of success as well as good health. Did you know that people even use green talismans for advancement in their career? In fact, even when yearning for potency; rehabilitation and protection from disease; green crystals are very helpful. Pink crystals are also helpful when it comes to the heart chakra.

Among the green crystals you could use are the emerald; malachite; aventurine; jade; peridot; moss agate; chrysoprase;

serpentine; green calcite; green tourmaline; dioptase; tree agate; bloodstone; fuchsite; epidote; moldavite; Rose quartz; and grossularite.

The best location for the green crystal is your chest because that is where your heart chakra happens to be. And you can enhance its performance by adding a pink crystal as well. The reason to get back up from pink is that pink is great at clearing negative emotions.

Blue crystals

The blue crystals correspond to the fifth chakra which is actually the throat chakra. These are the crystals that actually tag along patience; respect; trust; and even faith.

When you are in dire need of spiritual cleansing; or you are dealing with betrayal or even feelings of insecurity, blue crystals are great for you. And if your need is one of being guilt laden and you need absolution; or in cases where you simply need reconciliation, light blue crystals will work well.

Just place them on your breastbone; right at the lower end of your throat. Among the blue crystals you can choose include the turquoise; the blue quartz; the blue apatite; the sodalite; the blue lace agate; blue calcite; blue kyanite; the angelite; chrysocolla; dumortierite; the larimar; the blue opal; lapis lazuli; and even the Tanzanite.

Indigo crystals

In place of exact indigo, crystals that are dark blue in color can also be used. The indigo crystals correspond to the sixth chakra – the third eye mostly associated with high intelligence as well as psychic abilities.

Indigo crystals actually elevate your spiritual mastery and increase your wisdom. You need them for good judgment and mature handling of matters. And if you need to escape trickery and get lies revealed to you, these crystals can help. As for the ones that are light colored, they are capable of enhancing your gratefulness as well as modesty.

Great examples of indigo crystals include the azurite; purple fluorite; iolite; sugarlite; sodalite; and also the covellite. An indigo crystal is best placed on your forehead, the location of your third eye. In addition to the indigo crystals, you can add to your selection the amethyst or any other purple crystal.

Violet crystals

These crystals that correspond to your crown chakra are great in elevating your intuition as well as imagination. In fact, if you want to get inspired, violet crystals are the ones to go for. However, if there are some issues that remain a mystery to you and you would like that sorted out, it is advisable to go for those that are dark violet. Also, as far as the working of your crown chakra is concerned, crystals that are white or gold in color are also helpful.

Some of the crystals that enhance the working of your crown chakra include the vera cruz amethyst; charoite tumble stone; purple scapolite; Tanzanite crystals; pink lazurine; amegreen; violet-purple sugilite; cactus quartz; snow quartz; amber; diamond; moldavite; chevron; and even the violet purpurite.

Whatever violet crystal you select, the best location to place it is the top of your head where the crown chakra is located.

One thing you need to remember is that your crown chakra and your brow chakra work very closely. So just in case you chose a crystal from the amethyst cluster for your brow chakra, do not choose an amethyst for your crown chakra. Instead, you could choose, say, clear quartz to boost your crown chakra. And in case for your brow chakra you chose a dark blue crystal, then a violet one will do just fine for your crown chakra. Speaking of the clear quartz, this is one crystal you can program to boost the energies of any one of your crystals – it is that versatile.

Chapter 14:
Crystals That Require Special Handling

Who would not wish their crystals to last long and even be capable of being re-energized as normally as possible? Most crystals are not ordinary stones you stumble over on a daily basis. In fact, they are not like the pebbles you find on stream or river beds. That means even the price of most of them is far higher than that of a pumice stone. As is the norm with scarce, rare or pricey items, you will wish to safeguard the nature and integrity of your precious possessions – your crystals.

However, the fact is that some people have no idea what crystal is delicate and in what way it is delicate. And for those who know it, not everyone knows how best to handle those that are delicate. This is the information this chapter carries.

Again, some of those crystals you come across in shops may be great in healing and great as ornaments and decorations, but they may, at the same time, be potentially dangerous to you, the handler. When you buy a crystal, you surely do not want to get more than you bargained for. For that matter, it is important that you know which crystals are potentially harmful to you and in what manner. That way, you will know your limits when it comes to getting exposed to the crystals and also how to handle the crystals in order to suppress their potential danger. You will get that information too in this chapter.

List of sensitive crystals

Apatite

You know that crystal that is basically calcium phosphate with traces of fluorine and chlorine amongst other minor elements?

It is the apatite; something that you may often find in fertilizer manufacturing.

Nobody is trying to suggest that crystal users are based in laboratories, but still it is good to be aware that the apatite can get damaged by things that are acidic. Yet apatite comes in handy in bolstering the function of your throat chakra. All you need is to ensure your apatite does not get into contact with acid.

Amethyst

This crystal that is very much valued for its beauty is also held in high esteem in the field of crystal healing for its energy frequency. It works marvelous with your third eye as well as your crown chakra. Here we are talking of a crystal capable of elevating your level of intuition and matters spiritual.

However, it is significantly sensitive when it comes to direct sunlight. If ever you want to expose it to sunlight for the purpose of cleansing or even re-energizing, let it be for short spells. Long exposure to bright sunlight results in the crystal's color fading. Needless to say, the natural properties of a crystal have a lot to do with its healing abilities. So a faded amethyst cannot be said to be as effective as one that still has its natural color intact.

Calcite

Calcite crystals come in varieties and they are generally helpful to all your chakras. Calcites are generally sensitive to water and it may be a good idea to generally keep all the varieties out of water. You also need to know that they are susceptible to scratches. However, one variety, the one with resin, can withstand water, and you will know it by its smoothness and also waxy texture. That is the one known as rough calcite. Then there is the honey calcite that is averse to strong sunlight. You need to guard against exposing this variety to long periods of direct sunshine in order to protect the crystals from fading.

Fluorite

Fluorite is another crystal that easily scratches. And if that happens, you will begin to notice dullness, which is not a good thing for the crystal's performance. It is advisable to store fluorite crystals on their own because of that delicate aspect of them. It is also another of those crystals that fade when exposed to sunlight for lengthy periods – call it being photosensitive. You also need to take great care when handling the fluorite because its cleavage planes can easily fracture if they get hit. Remember that fluorite works well with both your heart chakra as well as your third eye.

Gypsum

Gypsum crystals work well with your crown chakra. However, they are sensitive to water and you therefore need to keep them dry. Some of them may actually absorb water while others may literally disintegrate after a period of being dull. Gypsums include selenite; satin spar; fishtale; among others.

Halite

This crystal that primarily works well with your heart chakra is also helpful to your sacral chakra. But you need to keep in mind that it is salt based and as you can guess it cannot survive in water without its texture being adversely affected. Even leaving it lying in damp places like in the cellar can have your halite crystal disintegrating.

Lapis Lazuli

The lapis lazuri works well with both your throat as well as brow chakras. And you need not worry much about it because the kind of sensitivity it has is unlikely to come into play when dealing with crystal healing. This crystal is actually sensitive to pressure.

Malachite

You need to know the sensitivities of this crystal whose dedication is to your heart chakra. The malachite is extra soft and hence susceptible to scratches. Sustained scratching then leads to dullness, something that is bound to affect the crystal's energy flow. It is, therefore, advisable to carry the malachite on its own to avoid it rubbing against other crystals. The sensitivity of the malachite also extends to heat; to hot water; and also to ammonia and acid.

Rose quartz

The Rose quartz is very helpful to your heart chakra. Some varieties of its varieties are sensitive to light and so need to be kept away from direct sunlight.. Long exposure causes these varieties to fade. And even when they are being re-charged, they need not be exposed to the sunlight for longer than a couple of hours. Since you may not always be able to tell which variety fades and which one does not, it is best to protect all Rose quartz from prolonged exposure to sunlight.

Turquoise

These crystals that help the workings of your throat chakra are actually messed up by moisture because of their soft and porous texture. They are also adversely affected when they get in touch with oil; perspiration; household detergents; and even cosmetics. In fact, you are advised to remove your ring if it is turquoise when working with water or even washing hands.

To be forewarned, as usual, is to be forearmed. There is no reason now why your crystals cannot last long and continue to be effective in improving your well being. The other important warning, of course, relates to the potential danger posed by some of these crystals – some very good in healing but still potentially dangerous. And those potential dangers have already been discussed in an earlier chapter here and the culprits pointed out.

When seeking the services of a therapist, be sure to distinguish the efficacy of your crystal from the efficiency of your therapist. A crystal healer who is not well versed with the various crystals in existence, how they work, their limitations and also their potential dangers, if any, cannot be helpful to you. He may even expose you to danger especially if handling a potentially harmful crystal. You may wish to get referral from a reliable friend who have been in contact with a good therapist. And, of course, you need not a recommendation at face value. Considering that crystals heal through energy vibrations, it is best that you speak with the recommended therapist before you commit to his or her services. If you get a negative vibe about the whole thing, it is advisable that you let that one go and seek someone else. Intuition plays a big role in matters of energy flow, including the vibrations and frequencies of all your energies – yours and those of the therapist.

Chapter 15:
How Crystals Target Specific Concerns or Chakras

Now that you understand the way crystals work and how you can use them, you can begin selecting your crystals according to your specific needs. Below, we'll review the seven chakras and the crystals that correspond with each.

Crystals for Balancing Chakras

The crown/seventh chakra

The colors that correspond with this chakra are violet and golden-white, so it makes sense that the crystals used to balance the crown chakra are amethyst, Oregon opal, and clear quartz. Some individuals also choose to use white calcite and white topaz near the seventh chakra. Diamond and sapphire are also popular choices for regulating the crown chakra's frequency.

The third eye/sixth chakra

Indigo is the third eye chakra's representative hue, so the crystals lapis lazuli, sugilite, and azurite all have beneficial powers when it comes to achieving harmony here. Sodalite and blue fluorite are other popular choices for regulating the sixth chakra.

The throat/fifth chakra

Recognized for its lighter blue corresponding color, the throat chakra has corresponding crystals which include sapphire, angelite, blue lace agate, and aquamarine. Blue turquoise, calcite, and kyanite are other common crystals that work to balance the fifth chakra.

The heart/fourth chakra

Deeply associated with love, the heart chakra has a wide variety of corresponding crystals. Rose quartz is among the most popular, while watermelon tourmaline, aventurine, and moonstone are other known matches. In addition, many green-hued crystals, including emerald, green calcite, jade, and green tourmaline, are beneficial for this chakra.

The solar plexus/third chakra

This chakra, which is associated with the color yellow, has corresponding crystals that include citrine, yellow jasper, amber, topaz, yellow sapphire, and golden calcite.

The sacral/second chakra

The most common corresponding crystals for this chakra are red jasper, red garnet, ruby, carnelian, and red and brown aventurine.

The root/first chakra

Known for its deep, red hue, the first chakra benefits from bloodstone, red zincite, tiger's eye, as well as obsidian, onyx, and hematite. Smoky quartz is another matching crystal for this chakra.

Crystals for Multiple Chakras

In addition to the crystals listed above, which correspond with one particular chakra, there are additional gems that serve other specific purposes, which we'll discuss below.

Aligning the chakras

There are certain gems that work well specifically for aligning or opening the chakras. In particular, you should choose to use chrysoprase, pink kunzite, and kyanite.

Cleansing the chakras

Moonstone and celestite effectively detoxify all of the chakras. Green fluorite also has renewal properties that benefit each chakra.

Stimulating chakra energy

Use clear or white calcite to rev your chakras' energy levels, especially near the crown. Malachite is a great stimulate that has the greatest impact on the heart and throat chakras. Turquoise can also elevate the vibrancies of all chakras.

Opening the chakras

Quartz crystal is an extremely popular choice for opening all of the chakras, especially for beginners. In fact, many crystal users keep quartz readily available to them at all times, and rely heavily on the wondrous benefits that this crystal offers.

Crystals that Target Specific Ailments and Issues

While using crystals to regulate specific chakras will benefit any ailments corresponding to those areas, you may still want to incorporate certain gemstones to heal recurring issues. If you experience any of the health troubles listed below, consider using the corresponding crystal to alleviate the problem. Keep in mind that you should still place the stone near the corresponding chakra from which the problem ιates, and that not all crystals work the same for everyone.

Recurring headaches

The stones that work best to heal chronic headaches and migraines are amethyst, turquoise, amber, and lapis lazuli. Headaches can also be a result of an imbalance between the solar plexus and head energies, so if you notice a mild upset stomach accompanying your headaches, consider using moonstone or citrine to resolve the issue.

Sleeplessness

Oftentimes, inability to sleep is a result of another issue. For example, if you are unable to sleep because of constant worrying or stress, you might want to consider using rose quartz, citrine, or amethyst to help promote restfulness. If, however, you're experiencing nightmares, you may want to employ protective stones such as smoky quartz and tourmaline. In addition to using these during your healing practice, you may also want to place them at the foot of your bed while you sleep. Labradorite can also promote sound sleep, since it aids in protecting against unpleasant thoughts or feelings.

Depleted energy

Most crystals with yellow, orange, and red hues will increase energy levels. The most powerful of these are deep red garnet and golden amber or topaz. If you're looking for motivation that you can apply to your everyday life for practical purposes, consider using crystals with deeper hues, such as tiger's eye and jasper. You can also boost your entire chakra system by holding a clear quartz crystal in each hand and pointing them upwards, while simultaneously keeping a citrine crystal on your solar plexus.

Lack of concentration

Using quartz crystals is perhaps one of the best ways to achieve mental clarity. You can also use amber and citrine to stimulate your memory, while lapis lazuli can amplify thoughts. Amethyst also promotes clarity, and can help you to become cognizant of your own specific goals. If you need to study for a big exam, consider using fluorite, which helps to enhance brain functionality.

Chapter 16: A Comprehensive List of Crystals and Gems and Their Purposes

Consult this list if you find yourself in a shop with gems or crystals, or if you are searching for some on the internet and don't know where to start. If you find yourself drawn to a crystal or gem, keep in mind that its purpose in your life may be greater than what it is specifically intended for. Although these are the commonly known benefits of specific crystals, using crystals or gems to heal yourself is beneficial in general. In other words, do not feel as if you must stick to a specific type of crystal or gem to target a certain issue that you may be experiencing. You can first seek out the crystal or gem that is intended to heal that issue, but always keep an open mind and explore other options if you are drawn towards them. Again, it's possible that your energy field will operate on a level that is greater than what your consciousness is able to understand, and your specific vibrations will benefit immensely from that of a gem or crystal that it is drawn to.

Still, if you are beginning your healing practice with crystals or gems, it is helpful to know what each type is most commonly used for. That way, you'll already be armed with knowledge before you go into a shop or look online. Although there are many more crystal and gem varieties in existence other than the ones we've listed here, these are among the most common and popular choices used in crystal healing. Use them in whichever method of crystal healing you prefer and feel most comfortable with. If desired, perform the laying of the stones with the crystals and gems, in conjunction with the corresponding chakras listed:

Abalone Shell

Best used for the solar plexus, heart, and throat chakras to enhance peace, communication, and beauty.

Agate

This crystal comes in a variety of colors, and each affects certain chakras differently. Blue lace agate works well to enhance stabilization and peacefulness, and can be used near the throat and third eye chakras. Black agate is commonly used for protection and grounding, and should be used in conjunction with the root chakra. Fire agate can help one achieve spiritual perfection and should be used near the solar plexus and root chakras. It, too, can be used to encourage protection, as well as vitality. White agate should be used near the crown chakra and calls upon stability, clarity, and grounding.

Alexandrite

This crystal is used to promote courage and self-esteem. It can also boost regeneration. For best results, use it near the heart and root chakras if performing the laying of the stones.

Amber

Use amber to promote clarity and protection. It is designed for use with the solar plexus chakra.

Amethyst

This popular purple gem works best to regulate the crown and third eye chakras. Use it to enhance your spirituality and protection, or to seek purification.

Angelite

If you are trying to pursue a higher sense of self or tap into your intuition, this is the crystal for you. Use it near your third eye, crown, or throat chakra.

Apache Tears

This unique crystal is used specifically for the purpose of forgiveness. It may also help to ground you or enhance your protection. Hone in on the root chakra when using this crystal.

Aquamarine

Works best for promoting communication and a sense of calmness. It can be used among the heart, throat, and third eye chakras.

Aragonite

This crystal is best-known for its grounding and centering capabilities. It should be used to balance the root, sacral, and crown chakras to enhance stability.

Aventurine

Aventurine is another type of crystal that comes in a variety of colors, each of which plays a different role in healing. Blue is used to foster empathy and understanding and should be used with the throat, crown, and third eye chakras. Brown aventurine is designated to promote a connection with the earth, and can also enhance prosperity and one's ability to learn. It should balance the root and solar plexus chakras. Green best works to enhance healing and growth, and should be placed near the heart. Orange aventurine is tied to luck, manifestation of one's dreams, and creativity. It can also be placed near the heart, but can benefit the sacral and solar plexus chakras as well. Pink fosters creativity as well, but has more of a calming effect than the other colors. Place pink aventurine near the heart. Red should be used with the root chakra and helps foster balance, along with creativity and prosperity. White aventurine can help to develop self-reflection and clarity. It can be used to balance all chakras. Yellow aventurine corresponds with detoxification and balance, and should be used with the sacral and solar plexus chakras.

Azurite

This beautiful blue crystal helps to develop one's ability to recognize his or her intuition. It is also linked with developing enhanced communication and guidance. Use it to balance the third eye, throat, and crown chakras.

Bloodstone

Bloodstone is most effective when used for detoxification and healing purposes. It can be used among many chakras, including the root, sacral, heart, and solar plexus.

Braziliantine

Use this stone if you're seeking insight, release, or the attainment of some goal or object. For best results, lay it on the solar plexus or heart chakras.

Bronzite

Best for protection and harmony. It can be used to balance all chakras.

Calcite

This crystal has different purposes depending on its color. Amber calcite enhances balance and provides support, especially within the crown, sacral, and solar plexus chakras. Blue calcite has more of a soothing effect and promotes emotional release. It is best used for the third eye and throat chakras. Brown can help to develop inner peace and motivation, and should be used specifically among the solar plexus chakra. Green calcite balances the heart chakra to foster healing and emotional balance. Orange can bring joy and creativity, especially when used with the root and sacral chakras. Pink calcite promotes universal love and compassion, and should therefore be used to balance the heart chakra. To develop self-confidence and hope, use yellow calcite among your solar plexus, crown, and sacral chakras.

Carnelian

If you need to enhance your physical vitality, select carnelian and use it with your sacral chakra.

Cavansite

Cavansite should be used by those seeking inspiration. It works best when used among the throat, heart, and third eye energy fields.

Celestite/Celestine

This very powerful crystal can be used to tap into spiritual communication. It is said to open the lines for angelic communication and divine expression, as well as overall clarity. To pursue these objectives, lay this stone near the throat, crown, and third eye chakras.

Chlorite (green)

This stone can be used to balance all chakras and remove negativity. It is also hailed for its healing and cleansing properties.

Citrine

Citrine is a well-known chakra cleanser. While it has the ability to cleanse all chakras, it can promote balance and abundance, especially when used in conjunction with the crown, solar plexus, and sacral chakras.

Copal

Commonly used to balance the solar plexus chakra. It instates healing, cleansing, and protection among the energy fields.

Copper

Use copper to amplify your energy levels or become more grounded. It can also help to balance your life. Place it near the root and sacral chakras for best results.

Creedite

If you are attempting to pursue astral projection, this stone is best suited to help your practice. It can also heighten your levels of vibration and foster your ability to express yourself. Use it with the throat and crown chakras.

Cuprite

Cuprite enhances strength and altruism. It is best used with the root chakra.

Cympophane (a.k.a. Cat's Eye)

Promotes success and prosperity and can also be used for protection. Place among heart and solar plexus chakras.

Danburite

In addition to providing a sense of universal love, danburite is credited with enhancing angelic vibration and leading to higher communication. It should be used with the heart chakra primarily, along with the third eye and crown.

Emerald

This crystal promotes a sense of hope among its users. It can also develop prosperity and aid in healing processes. Emerald is most effective when used with the heart chakra.

Eudialyte

Use eudialyte if you are seeking self-acceptance. It will also foster a sense of release and trust. The heart and root chakras benefit most from this crystal.

Feldspar

Feldspar can be used among a variety of chakras to help individuals cope with a situation. It encourages positive thinking and self-esteem.

Fluorite

Like many other popular crystals, fluorite comes in many colors. Blue fluorite fosters inner peace and should be used near the throat and third eye chakras. Green fluorite can heal, cleanse, and energize, and works best with theheart and throat chakras. Purple fluorite corresponds with the crown and third eye chakras to develop intuition and creativity, as well as focus. Rainbow fluorite can be used in correspondence with a number of chakras, including the heart, third eye, throat, and crown. It helps to stabilizeand ground an individual, and also leads to harmony.

Fuchsite

Use this crystal with the heart chakra for healing and rejuvenation.

Galena

To use galena, place it near the root chakra. It can promote harmony and balance, and help to ground you.

Garnet

If you are hoping to improve your relationships, use garnet to enhance love, commitment, and loyalty. While it works well to balance the heart chakra, it can also be used with the root and sacral chakras.

Gold

It may cost you more than most gems and crystals, but gold has great powers for enhancing attraction and amplification. It can also promote regeneration. Use it with the sacral, heart, and solar plexus chakras for best results.

Halite

This crystal is credited with purifying and cleansing the energy field. Use it near your heart and sacral chakras.

Hematite

If you need to ground or detoxify your vibrations, use hematite, specifically for your root chakra.

Herkimer Diamond

Use this crystal near the third eye and crown chakras to receive a sense of peace, or if you need to release any unwanted negativity. It can also be used to achieve attunement.

Hiddenite (a.k.a. green spodumene)

To receive the benefit of this stone, lay it near your heart chakra. You'll promote unconditional love, gratitude, and hope as a result.

Howlite

This universally beneficial gem can be used in conjunction with all of the chakra energy fields. It will bestow a sense of calm upon you and heighten your spirituality and awareness.

Jade

This popular green gem is known for its ability to enhance prosperity and longevity. Use it with your root and heart chakras for best results.

Jasper

If you're suffering from a creative block, use jasper to call upon inspiration. Additionally, it can offer protection and balance. There are a few different varieties of jasper, and each has its own strengths. For example, black jasper is best for promoting honesty and balance, especially when used to balance the root and solar plexus chakras. Bumble bee jasper aids in creative processes, and should be used near the solar plexus and sacral chakras. The unique Dalmatian jasper can ward off negativity and offer protection. Use it near the sacral, root, and solar plexus chakras for maximum benefits. If you are struggling through a difficult endeavor, rely on fancy jasper for perseverance and discipline, and apply it to your solar plexus and root chakras. Leopard skin jasper can foster your desire for journeying and will also offer protection. It works especially well with the root, crown, and heart chakras. Mookaite jasper instills awareness and helps you tap into your intuition, especially when used for the sacral, solar plexus, and root chakras. The beautiful picture jasper gem does wonders for boosting confidence and creative sparks, so use it with your third eye and root chakras. Red jasper should be used for stabilityand nurturing, especially in balancing the root and sacral chakras. Striped brown jasper can comfort and center you, and works best with the root chakra. If you need to reconnect with Mother Earth and detoxify any aspect of your existence, seek out yellow jasper and perform the laying of the stones on your solar plexus. Finally,zebra jasper also offers a connection to Mother Earth, along with additional joy and optimism. It should be used with the root chakra.

Kunzite

Use kunzite to achieve divine and unconditional love. It should be used in relation to your heart chakra.

Kyanite

Like many other common gemstones, kyanite can be found in a few different colors and variations. Black kyanite can align and repair all chakras, but is especially advantageous for promoting manifestation and aiding in meditation when used with theroot chakra. Blue kyanite can raise your vibrations and allow you to hone in on your dreams. It can also be used for aligning all chakras but works best with the third eye and throat. Green kyanite fosters personal development and opens the lines for spiritual communication. Use it with the heart chakra for best results. If you need to enhance your self-esteem or imagination, use orange kyanite to balance your sacral chakra.

Labradorite

Should you ever need to undergo a major transformation, you can rely on labradorite to guide you through. It can also provide strength and a link to your intuition. Use it with your third eye and crown chakras.

Lapis lazuli

Find inner power with this gem. Best used with the throat, third eye, and crown.

Lepidolite

Transitioning can be eased with the use of lepidolite, especially when used to balance the crown, third eye, heart, and throat chakras.

Magnesite

If you ever need assistance while meditating, you may want to select magnesite to aid you in your practice. It can offer the ability to find peace and ease visualization processes. When performing the laying of the stones, place magnesite near your crown, third eye, and heart chakras.

Malachite

This unique stone can be used to amplify or heal. Use it with the heart, third eye, and throat chakras.

Manganese with sugilite

Used to promote cooperation and creativity, mangagnese with sugilite can be especially beneficial when used in workplace settings. It can also be most beneficial when used to balance the heart chakra.

Mexican fire opal

To call upon ancient wisdom, use Mexican fire opal when balancing your sacral chakra. It can also be used to center your energy and provide patience.

Moonstone

Become the recipient of goddess energy by using moonstone in your crystal healing practice. You'll become more inspired and in tune with your intuition. Be sure to focus on your sacral, third eye, and crown chakras.

Moqui Marbles

Use these with in conjunction with the root chakra to achieve protection and to become more grounded or centered.

Morganite

In addition to helping one find a greater sense of joy, morganite can enhance a person's ability to achieve angelic communication and find divine love. It should be used with the heart and crown chakras.

Muscovite

Best used with the heart chakra, muscovite can provide strength and help facilitate learning. Gold star muscovite can specifically enhance a person's learning capabilities and communication processes. It, too, should be used to balance the heart chakra.

Obsidian

While many individuals are most familiar with black obsidian, there are a few different varieties of the popular stone, each of which can be used for crystal healing. Black obsidian should be used to protect and heal, balancing the root chakra. Mahogany can clear blockages and ground your energy levels. It can also be used for the root chakra, as well as the sacral chakra. The unique rainbow chakra is linked to happiness and should be used to regulate the root chakra. Snowflake obsidian can provide support or balance and is most effectivewhen laid near the root, solar plexus, and sacral chakras.

Onyx

Onyx can regulate the root chakra and can provide strength in times of need. It is also beneficial for evoking protection.

Opal

There are two main kinds of opal that can be used for crystal healing. In specific, blue opal calls upon creativity and courage, and should be used with the throat chakra. Pink opal, on the other hand, can provide joy and renewal, as well as insight to certain situations. Use it with the heart chakra for best results.

Petrified Wood

Use this popular stone when you need to become more grounded. It can evoke strengthand support, and is best used for balancing the sacral and root chakras.

Phosphosiderite

In times of need, phosphosiderite can create hope and encourage healing processes. It is also linked with enabling a heightened sense of spirituality. Use it with the heart and third eye chakra.

Pyrite

To ward off negativity, use pyrite in your crystal healing practice. For some, it may also bring greater prosperity and protection. It can be conveniently used among all chakras for benefit.

Quartz

Perhaps the most common crystal used for healing, quartz is available in a wide variety of options. Because it is one of the most prevalent crystals in the healing practice, it can be beneficial to know what each type is used for. Aqua aura quartz is used to channel emotions and raise spiritual awareness. It should be placed among the heart, throat, third eye, and crown chakras. Blue quartz can provide a sense of clarity. It may also open up communication to give way to deeper, more meaningful connections. Use it with the throat and third eye chakras for best results. Champagne aura quartz, also known as smokey aura, can help find solutions to issues or deflate conflict. It can be used to benefit the sacral, solar plexus, heart, throat, third eye, and crown chakras. Chromium quartz is most advantageous for theheart chakra, and evokes joy and balance. One of the most commonly used crystals in the art of healing is the clear quartz, which benefits all chakras. It can heal, amplify, and enhance specific facets of your life for a better, more harmonious existence. Green quartz promotes abundance and creativity. It can also conjure empathy, and should be used in conjunction with the heart chakra. Hematoid (or harlequin) quartz boosts concentration and self-esteem. For best results, pair it with the sacral, solar plexus, or root energy fields. If you are interested in conjuring psychic visions, opening the lines to spiritual communications, or producing more vivid dreams, then employ indigo aura quartz in your crystal healing practice. It should be placed near the topmost chakras, including the throat, third eye, and crown. Iris quartz can promote reconciliation, so use it if you are hoping to make up with someone. It will also provide you with the strength and optimism you need to do so, and can be used among all chakras. Lemon quartz will heighten your energy levels and can be used to balance the solar plexus chakra. If you are suffering from anxiety, you may want to consider implementing lithium quartz in your practice. This is also one of the best-known healing crystals available. It can be used to balance all of the chakras and is said to be advantageous for all types of individuals, especially when it comes to finding emotional peace. Peach quartz has the ability to provide vitality and free-flowing energy; be sure to use it for the sacral and solar plexus chakras. Phantom quartz can enhance spiritualgrowth and transformation, and is also used for raising universal awareness. Like many quartz crystals, it can be used to regulate all of the chakras. Rainbow aura quartz is another powerful healer. It works very well when used during meditation and can also promote communication. Use it with the heart, third eye, and crown chakras. Rose quartz is famous for its ability to conjure love, and is also helpful for promoting compassion and self-esteem. Thus, it should be used to balance the heart chakra. Smokey quartz can ward off negativity and help ground an individual. It should be used with the root and solar plexus chakras. The beautiful white snow quartz can help to create peace and clarity, and works best with the crown chakra. Strawberry quartz will amplify your intentions and provide a deeper understanding for any issues you are experiencing, especially when balancing the heart chakra. Finally, tangerine quartz can help you find acceptance. It also promotes growth and regulates the sacral, solar plexus, and root chakras.

Ruby

This heavily pigmented gem should be consulted if you are seeking love and passion. Thus, it can be used for regulating the heart chakra. It may also be used with the root chakra.

Sandstone

Best used for the sacral chakra, sandstone enhances creativity and clarity.

Sapphire

This beautiful stone is often thought of as being blue in color, but it is also available in other varieties. The well-known blue sapphire should be used to balance throat, third eye, and crown chakras, and will offer wisdom and prosperity. Pink sapphire has been said to evoke clairvoyance and general spiritual enlightenment, as well as love. Use it with your heart chakra. Star sapphire may connect individuals with higher beings, and can provide stabilizing thoughts that will lead to clarity. Use it with your throat and third eye chakras for best results. Violet sapphire is the best of all for healing, and should be designated to balancing the crown and third eye chakras.

Silver

This shimmering stone will help to balance any chakra, and can even work on aligning your entire energy field. It is also beneficial for achieving manifestation and attraction, and may even improve your ability to follow your intuition.

Sodalite

Use this gem to focus your energy or whenever you need some guidance. It works best with the third eye and throat chakras.

Tiger Eye (red)

Use it with your root chakra to enhance vitality and motivation.

Topaz

This stone can enhance your awareness and creativity. Blue topaz works best with the throat and third eye chakras, while imperial topaz is better for the solar plexus and crown chakras to achieve manifestation and divine guidance.

Turquoise

This gem isn't just beautiful in color; it's also is known for its healing powers and evoking strong communication and release. It should be used to balance the throat and third eye chakras for best results.

Chapter 17:
Short-cut to Identifying the Crystal You Need

In some cultures, including some in Africa, they say you need not build your house like your neighbor's. And it makes sense because your needs are not necessarily like those of your neighbor's. And, of course, the English keep warning you against copying the Joneses.

In the same vein, crystals are varied in look, make-up and natural power; and you also have your personal needs that could be different from those of everyone else. So would it make sense to pick a crystal from a shop just because that is what your friend bought? Of course not! In any case, with the potent information on crystals that you already have, you know that crystals have more importance beyond their aesthetic value. The challenge is that you may know your need but find it difficult to make up your mind the best crystal to buy or even the best range of crystals to choose from for your particular need.

Here are some common needs that people seek to satisfy, plus their corresponding crystals:

Money related needs

There are those crystals whose energies are geared towards attracting prosperity and those are the ones you need here. And, of course, these ones contribute towards clearing your root chakra whose energy is geared towards prosperity.

Another thing you need to keep in mind is that a crystal is not necessarily good for a singular purpose. Just like whole wheat serves to provide you with protein, energy and fiber, so do some crystals serve a number of purposes.

Below is a great choice of crystals for money matters:

Citrine

Brings you the dollar and also keeps you lucky and protected.

Garnet

Attracts wealth as well as love.

Malachite

In addition to attracting the dollar, it also brings you love and keeps you protected.

Smokey Quartz

This one enhances your power on top of attracting wealth.

Ametrine

In addition to deleting the word poverty from your vocabulary, this crystal brings you power.

Aventurine

This one brings in money plus lots of good luck

Topaz

This is one rich crystal as beyond the money, it also brings you healing; protection; love; and also power.

Fire Opal

This one attracts money like a magnet, alright. And it is also great for healing as well as protection

Green Calcite

You will get the money through this crystal and on top of that great healing

Jade

Here is another rich crystal that will not just attract wealth but also great healing; love; and also protection. It helps you develop a positive attitude towards acquisition of money while you relate that to what you need to accomplish with the money.

Green Tourmaline

Through this crystal you will see the money; then relish the abundance of power; love; and also healing

Tree Agate

This is also one to add power and healing to the money. The caution here is that this crystal requires patience in its working.

Chrysanthemum stone

This crystal attracts the dollar; then on top of that makes you one lucky crystal bearer; and brings you power and love. To bring in the money, it begins by altering your attitude to one of positive thinking.

Sapphire

This one is great for wealth; but on top of the money it also attracts love and brings you healing

Love Matters

Hearts have been broken and sometimes love is evasive. And sometimes also people try all sorts of methods to make love happen. Some ways work, others backfire, while still others turn out to be ridiculous jokes. Now here are crystals that link up with your fourth chakra, which incidentally is your heart chakra, and the energies flow in such a manner as to kind of increase your propensity to love and be loved.

Any of the following crystals is great for your love life:

Lithium Quartz

This one also enhances your power and brings you healing on top of attracting love

Mangano Calcite

On top of enhancing your love life, this one too enhances your power and brings you healing as well

Scolecite

This adds power to its love feather

Charoite

This one helps you in matters of love alright, but also in matters of healing; protection; as well as power

Prehnite

This is another crystal that adds to the love property the great properties of healing; protection; and also power

Emerald

Beyond enriching your love life, the emerald brings you lots of healing

Hematite

On top of the love, the hematite brings you healing as well as protection

Jade

Rich as the jade is in love, it is also great for healing as well as power

Malachite

This crystal is very valuable because even as it brings you love it also brings in the money and much needed protection

Rainbow Jasper

This is great for love as well as healing

Rhodonite

This too is for love as well as healing

Rose Quartz

In addition to your rose quartz bringing you love, it also gives you healing

Turquoise

Not only does the turquoise crystal bring you love; it also enhances your protection and brings you good luck

Lepidolite

This is rich in properties; on top of love bringing you power and protections as well as good luck

Blue Quartz

This one brings you power on top of love

Moonstone

The moonstone is one rich crystal as on top of love it also enhances your healing; brings you power; and also makes you one lucky crystal bearer.

Blue Calcite

This one is not just good for love but also power and healing

Larimar

You can use this one, not just for matters of love, but also for healing as well as power.

Kunzite

Above the love this crystal brings into your life, you will be lucky and enjoy power and healing.

Imperial Topaz

This one will not just bring you love but money as well.

Chapter 18:
Different Love Situations call for Different Crystals

All work without play makes Jack a dull boy – obviously, universally accepted. So Jack needs to play. Does that mean that Jack has one outfit for all forms of recreation? Of course, not! There must be one suitable for swimming; another fit for the gym; and so on.

Likewise, you need to appreciate that matters pertaining to love come in all shapes and forms, so to speak; and as such, you need to know the best suitable natural crystals for each form of need.

For example:

- You may need to begin experiencing genuine love and romance

- Your wish may be to make an existing relationship better

- You may wish to rekindle dying or even lost love

- You may want to increase your capacity to love

- You may even want to improve on your marriage

- Your wish may be to meet your special someone or soul mate

Looking for Love

A bid to attract love

The best crystal for you for the sake of attracting love is the Rose Quartz.

And how do you use it? Go to the jeweler's shop and keep looking at it? Definitely, no – you will not bring your life to a halt just because you are seeking love. There are more convenient ways as these ones below:

- Place your rose quartz crystal at a location where you particularly need love flowing in. If it is in a crystal ball in your bedroom, that is fine; in the living room, that is fine too. Remember here we are talking of love in general and this rose quartz will work even when you want it to bring the members of your family or even your roommates closer.

- Make use of a rose quartz wand to draw your soul mate

Here we are thinking of you using the wand in a love spell ritual

- Place your rose quartz crystal right under your pillow

The effect of this is to draw towards you the love of the person you dream of

- Using a rose quartz that is heart shaped

This is another one of those that you use in a love ritual too to attract love

- Using a rose quartz crystal in egg shape

This one intensifies the love between you and your lover and attracts fertility too

- Wearing a rose quartz crystal as jewelry

By wearing the rose crystal on you, your self-love intensifies and you also get to attract more love towards you

Stabilizing an existing relationship that happens to be rocky

For this purpose, you use the rose quartz crystal in combination with another suitable crystal – in this case, the chrysocolla crystal. It is best that you place your chrysocolla crystal in either a red or even pink container that is partly filled with water. It is a beautiful crystal that also brings you healing; great calmness; and reduces the resistance within your body.

A bid to overcome jealousy

For this purpose, you use your rose quartz plus a chrysoprase crystal. This additional crystal has the effect of reducing your restlessness; making you see whatever issue you have with more clarity; and giving you hope while, at the same time, enhancing your joy.

To be able to embrace new experiences

When you want to do what they call, let go and move on, you use your rose crystal quartz together with either a peridot crystal or an azurite. The peridot, which, incidentally, was given prominence in the Holy Bible, and which has traditionally been worn by Catholic Bishops, helps to clear your mind and bar any negative emotions from influencing your thinking. As for the azurite, in addition to its healing properties, it enhances your intuition as well as inspiration.

Trying to come out of your shell

At times you may feel like your introverted nature is not doing you any good in matters of love and you wish to become more of an extrovert. In such situations, you use the rose quartz together with an imperial topaz or even citrine. The imperial topaz crystal serves to raise your self confidence and give you charisma.

Getting rid of fear or even apprehensionin matters of love

When such troubles abound, the crystal to use together with your rose quartz is the watermelon tourmaline. This combination of crystals is heavy duty because this rare crystal, watermelon tourmaline, in its green, pink and white colors all in the same crystal, brings you great love devoid of guilt; soothing your soul and balancing your masculine and feminine energies within you; and making you feel in harmony with life forces.

Seeking to Renew Love

Moonstone is your crystal to rekindle the flames in your relationship. It is known for boosting passion and enhancing romance. This stone is associated with the Roman goddess named Diana, who symbolizes fertility; freedom; abundance; providence; and also nature.

How to make the moonstone helpful in matters of love:

- Placing your moonstone sphere or even wand next to your bed

- Holding your moonstone crystal in your hand and then visualizing your lover in deep passion

- Wearing your moonstone crystal in form of jewelry

- Presenting your lover with a moonstone crystal that you have well cleaned of all divergent energies.

Here are varying situations where you can make good use of your moonlight crystal in combination with other supportive crystals:

Elevating your sexual energy levels and making you more attractive

The best combination here is the moonstone plus the sunstone. They are said to harmonize their energies to bring you both the influences of the sun and the moon. As such you are able to enjoy love; peace; spirituality; and overall success in your search.

Making you be more spontaneous with your lover

For this purpose, you need to combine the use of the moonlight crystal with rhodochrosite. The rhodochrosite crystal has capability of enhancing your intuition and soothing your heart; boosting your creativity; even as it elicits warm feelings from deep down your heart. Actually with this combination of crystals, your sensual feelings will be enhanced, and if necessary, you will find it easy to be erotic.

Healing emotional scars gotten from relationships of the past

The apt advice is to combine your moonstone crystal with rhodonite. Whereas your moonstone will do what it does best, and that is give you a great fresh beginning, the rhodonite crystal will play rescue. If you want something that overwhelms you with relaxation and gets you embracing love in whole, rhodonite is it. Its vibrations are all about love.

Chapter 19:
Guiding a Layman to Select Crystals for Common Ailments

What makes you sick anyway? As a matter of fact, very few of the ailments you suffer are congenital. Many are those that just invade you because your immune system has been compromised. The question is: Compromised by whom or by what? For now, you will be able to learn about the what-part and not the culprits as this is not the forum to explore how people can cast evil spells on you and get you ill.

Rather, you will see how your natural vibrations are interfered with and your energy flow through your chakras marred in a way that gets you feeling unwell, lethargic and devoid of motivation. Some of the things that can make you susceptible to disease include:

Negative thoughts

These ones mainly come in form of persistent anger as well as hate.

Environmental factors

You may be a victim of aerial pollution; pesticides; destabilizing electromagnetic waves; and such other unfriendly exposure.

From these then you find yourself catching common colds; allergies; eczema; asthma; or getting an infection of one kind or another. Now, apart from eating healthy and doing your part in exercising, another way of keeping your immune system strong and your body ready to ward off common ailments is by use of crystals. And since you do not want your house looking like an isle of rocks, you cannot assemble all the crystals that you know in your home. Nor can you go carrying kilos of crystals in your pockets – that would be insane; and yet what we are seeking in healing is sanity.

Just as you ensure you have antihistamines in your first aid box when you are prone to allergies; or anti acids when ulcers are known to give you unexpected pangs, so is it a good idea to have with you particular crystals for your particular health weakness. That way, you may even avoid that pill popping tendency that often ends up curing this and provoking that other ailment.

Here are some crystals and the ailments that they target:

Amber

Amber acts as an antibiotic; curing different infections. It also brings down your fever. It also has this ability to absorb pain so you feel relieved. You can use it also to heal your wounds. At a psychological level, it brings down your stress levels and gets you out of any emotional turmoil you may be in. On the overall, having amber with you makes you joyful and self confident.

And you know the best way to use it as a cure? Easy – you just apply it at the nape of your neck; on the inside part of your wrists; or even on your abdomen to target your solar plexus. Mark you this is a crystal that you can safely use on children particularly for its warm and luminous energies.

Amethyst

Do you feel unsettled in your stomach; plagued with insomnia; and all round restless? Amethyst is your crystal. It will cleanse your vital organs; regulate the flora along your intestines;

leaving you with a well streamlined immune system. Amethyst is capable of relieving you of stress and dealing effectively with any nervous disorders you may have.

When you have amethyst consistently with you, there is that natural tranquility that comes into your life. And so you begin to enjoy restful sleep and you stop being weighed down by negative feelings of anger and anxiety. Of course, as you know, when you sleep well you give your body time to recuperate and rejuvenate.

Ametrine

Look at this as coming from the chemist with an antibiotic and a tranquilizer, all to be taken simultaneously. Ametrine is a combination of both amethyst and citrine. And what that combination does is bring the healing properties of each crystal and make your healing more effective and faster. So ametrine clears your body of harmful toxins; your psyche of all negativity. What effectively happens then is that your fatigue goes away and you no longer feel depressed.

Aquamarine

Do you suffer allergies; sinus issues; throat infections; or even asthma? If so, you have a cure in aquamarine. And just so that you can enhance its effectiveness and speed of working, it is suggested that you use it together with the emerald crystal. You will be busting flu like you have never done before.

Calcite

If you can get hold of the green calcite crystal, it is all the better for your health. What happens is that calcite enhances your calcium absorption, which in turn stimulates growth. And you can deduce from this then that it is a crystal suitable for kids – they are the ones who are still growing, not you. For you, though, it can be calming to your mind, which is a good thing because that means less stress and anxiety; two conditions that can lead you to depression if unchecked.

Emerald

This crystal is a boost to your immune system. It helps the cells in your physical body to regenerate appropriately, and this is how your healing process hastens when you have had infections. You need the emerald a lot particularly when you consider that it is not always that you feed your body consistently well as to keep it protected from disease. Someone with the emerald is rarely emotionally low as the crystal gives you a general sense of balance – emotionally; physically; and even mentally.

Lepidolite

Do you have sleep disorders? Lepidolite is the crystal to alleviate those. You do not want to begin walking absent mindedly and losing concentration simply because you cannot sleep well. And, of course, your body needs consistent healthy rest to be able to regain its balance. So, for regular good night sleep; elimination of mood swings and stress related issues, you can use lepidolite.

Fluorite

This is one crystal you can use as anti-viral agent, particularly in its elixir form.

Others

The above list of the crystals that you can use for healing common ailments is not by any means exhaustive, but it shows

you those crystals that you can pick on with certainty and
without ambiguity as to what condition it is capable of
addressing.

Other crystals that play a part in boosting your immune
system and making you have a sense of well being include:

- Aqua aura quartz

- Aragonite

- Chalcedony

- Chiastolite

Chapter 20:
Right Way of Handling Healing Crystals

What good thing does not require maintenance? Even a car, when in storage, needs occasional starting up to ensure the piston and other car parts do not get stuck the next time you need to get the car out of the garage and back to normal use. This is the same case with crystals. Whether you are donning them as jewelry; placing them somewhere in your home or office; or simply keeping them in safe custody; there are some things you need to do to ensure they retain their energy and level of energy vibrations. Without good maintenance, you may as well begin viewing your crystals like any other stones with not much effect on your health and your welfare in general.

Why the special handling?

The importance of healing crystals is, clearly, not in their shape or size but in their energy levels and thus the level in which they can impact your life. When mined or prepared for commercial purposes, not much care is taken beyond ensuring they do not disfigured or get discolored. Yet there are other ways crystals can be messed up – by imparting negative energies into them. Movement of energy in organisms and objects is normally two-way. You can give out energy and impact people and objects around you and you can receive energy from other people and objects and be influenced by those energies. If the energy happens to be positive, that's good for you; but woe unto you if it happens to be negative.

Pertinent questions:

- Did the people doing the mining or collection of the crystals impart to them positive or negative energy?

- Did those doing the cutting of the pieces for adornment or for sale impart to them positive or negative energy?

- How about all those salespeople who handled your crystals before you acquired them – were they people of high positive energy or right the opposite?

Sincere answer is that you have no clue the kind of energy those people had and how much of it they imparted to the crystals that are now in your possession. But one thing is for sure – that crystals are extra sensitive and they easily transmit as well as receive energy.

Here are some steps you need to take to get your crystals ready for use:

- Cleansing them of any foreign bodies that may have attached themselves onto them

- Clearing them to ensure that any negative energy they may have absorbed from people handling them is out

- Re-aligning them accordingly so that their original vibrations and frequencies are reinstated.

How to Clean Your Crystals and Clear Them of Harmful Energies

Using sea salts

Seas salts are effective ingredients when you dissolve them in water, but you can only use them on crystals that are not brittle. You can let your crystals rest in the salted water overnight, possibly having added sage; basil; or even lavender into that cleaning water.

Using running water

This is as plain as it sounds – just putting your crystal under a water tap and letting the water run over it as you focus on it. In the meantime, you put forth a prayer to the Universe that its energy removes any negativity that may be in that crystal. During your cleaning of the crystal, it may even help to let yourself visualize some ray surrounding your crystal and imparting wisdom to it.

Using cleansing crystals

Here you pick one or some of the crystals known to sap out negative energy from others, and then enclose in the same container your other healing crystals are. Crystals with the power to cleanse others include the carnelian as well as clear quartz.

Smudging your crystals

In this method, sage comes in handy. Not only can you use it to clear negative energy in your crystals, but you can use it to clear stagnant energy from crystals you have been having. Smudging time is a great time to direct your intention towards your crystal.

Using a crystal cleaner

You need to keep this method till you have no alternative among the organic ways of cleaning. Mostly the times you are called upon to use this cleaner is when the crystals you want to clean are kind of porous – the kind that would dissolve in water. And in this case what you do is just use a couple of drops of crystal cleaner and you will have your crystals glittering. Example of such a crystal is the turquoise as it is porous.

Exactly what sensitivities do some crystals have?

Porosity

As mentioned earlier on, some crystals cannot get moist without getting destroyed. That is why you can only use other cleansing methods other than letting water run over them. In this regard, you need to take particular care on:

- The azurite; the halite; and the selenites because they are literally water soluble

- The lapis lazuli; the opal and also the turquoise as they are porous. With these ones, water is not exactly out of question, only that you cannot soak the crystals in it. So you can wipe them with something moist and then ensure you instantly dry them after the cleaning.

- As for the malachite, you need to use only cool water to clean it and then you instantly dry it afterwards.

Light sensitivity

Some crystals may fade if exposed to light for too long. The ones that stand out in this regard are:

- The amethyst as well as the Rose Quartz

- The turquoise as it may just dry out

Heat sensitivity

Some crystals are disfigured when exposed to heat. These include:

- The amethyst, which, in mild heat, begins to fade. In fact, in extreme heat the amethyst practically loses all its color and turns colorless.

- The quartz, which tends to fracture when temperatures around it are fluctuating

- The lapis lazuli, which cannot take extreme heat

- The malachite, like the quartz, does not fare well when exposed to fluctuating heat conditions

- Tourmaline, which gets its color marred in extreme heat

- Turquoise, which fares badly under heat in general.

Sensitivity to scratching

In this category are all crystals that are metallic or are on a mineral nature. By name, you have the Calcite; the Celestite; malachite; Fluorite; the Rhodochrosite; the Apatite; and the Lapis Lazuli. There are also sodalite; selenite; turquoise; hematite; as well as the moonstone.

Is this the complete process of preparing healing crystals?

Answer – no. You need to dedicate them; program them; activate them; and also charge them. By the time you are through with the process, your healing crystals will be clear energy channels and will be in the best of conditions to help in healing.

How to dedicate healing crystals

- Dedicating healing crystals basically means affirming to them that nothing short of positive energy will penetrate them.

- You will be making a commitment that you are going to see to it that the crystals are used only for good and never for anything evil.

- Note that you need to have your full focus on those crystals that you are dedicating, as you make those commitments.

The impact of your dedication is:

- To ensure that no negative energy clings to your crystals at the time of dedication and thereafter.

- To ensure that nobody and nothing will manage to interfere with the positive energy of your crystals, and as such the crystals will be protected from all negative influences.

Crystal Dedication Procedure

- Seek out a quiet place and sit down

- Have your crystals safely cupped in your hands as you sit

- Close your eyes

- Embark on taking deep, slow but regular breaths

- You know why you are undertaking this procedure, so focus on your crystals accordingly, even with your eyes closed. This means that you are making a deliberate effort to focus your inner energy on your crystals.

- In the quiet, allow yourself to sense the energy from your crystals

- Visualize some bright white ray beaming from the world around you and engulfing your crystals

- Visualize Mother Earth's own golden energy, with all its grounding properties, surrounding your crystals

- Visualize both energies merging and swirling together in harmony and having the effect of giving each other balance.

- Feel the positive energy and abundance of love filling you up

- Now allow yourself to direct that intense love to your crystals

- It is now time to make a focused statement of intent in your mind – so declare in deep commitment that those crystals you are holding will be used only for the utmost good.

- After that statement you may open your eyes. Look at your crystals and focus on them.

- With your eyes open and your focus still on the crystals, do repeat the mental commitment that you made a while before of using the crystals only for the utmost good.

- To bring your dedication to due conclusion, say: *May it be so.*

The next thing is programming your crystals

Why do you want to have crystals in your possession, whether to wear as jewelry, use to decorate your house or even place in hidden strategic places within your home? Well, the answer to that question is what guides you in programming the crystals. In programming your crystal, you are effectively making your intention or intentions get ingrained within your crystal. Remember as already mentioned, crystals are capable of absorbing energy the same way they emit energy. Some of the intentions people have when they program their crystals include:

- Healing purposes

- Seeking protection

- Seeking spiritual guidance

- Attracting more love in your life

- Seeking prosperity

- Seeking to create harmony in your home or even working place

The list of intentions you could have can be much longer, but the most important thing to note is that a single crystal can bear more than one intention. That means that the same crystal you are programming to help you heal physically can be programmed to bring harmony into your home.

It is advisable to limit your intentions to four or even five when programming your crystals. And the good thing is that as long as you do not reprogram those crystals thereafter, or even clear them of the original intentions, those intentions remain intact and your crystals continue to serve you as you originally intended.

Crystal programming procedure

The presumption here is that you have already cleansed your crystals – cleansing must always precede programming.

Have your intention ready. Of paramount importance here is to avoid ambiguity or any confusion. If you frame your intention in a way that leaves it subject to different interpretations, it will be the same kind of confusion you will be transferring to your crystals. The energy in your crystals will only help your cause properly if the wording of your intention is specific and clear. That way the crystal energies will be focused and correctly directed.

The other important thing is that you need to guard against going wild. The implication here is that you just can't pick any crystal and begin assigning it intentions irrespective of its energy intensity and vibrations. Already it has been pointed out in this book that certain crystals are suitable for certain issues. Remember when it comes to personal issues, you have chakras working in tandem with your chosen crystals. All these are important factors you need to consider lest you go against the grain and achieve little success from otherwise great and precious crystals.

Just for example, if your intention is to calm your nerves and your environment, you will be better off programming an aquamarine or chrysocolla; or even any one of the green stones – or blue ones. And if you need your crystal to bring stimulation within and around you, you will be better off programming a ruby, a garnet, or any of the red crystals. Of course, if you want tempered stimulation you could go for the orange or even yellow crystals; say a carnelian or even a piece of citrine.

The steps you take in programming your crystals

Just as in the cleansing procedure, you need to be in a quiet place with your mind fully focused on the intention you have for your crystals.

- Cozily hold your crystal in your hands

- Focus you gaze on the crystals

- Allow your energy to flow freely towards the crystals as you positively sense the energy from the crystals getting attuned to it

- You will reach a point where you and the crystals are in harmony with each other

- This is the instance to state the intention you have for the crystals – this time verbalizing it aloud. Remember clarity of intention is fundamental.

- You don't have to assume your crystals are programmed after stating your intention or intentions just once. A repeat process may be helpful. In fact, you are advised to repeat your intention a couple of times until your intuition tells you that the programming is well done.

Ways to Activate As Well As Re-Energize Your Crystals

Just as in cleaning, you need to be conscious which crystals are delicate, which ones are porous, which are those that can easily fade and so on. That way you will choose the best and safest method to activate and re-energize each set of crystals. And, of course, any crystal that is metallic, porous or with some water content will fare badly if soaked in salty water.

Crystals that you should not soak in salty water include the angelite; the calcite; the carnelian; hematite; lapis lazuli; the labradorite; the lodestone; marbles; moldavite; the opal; pearls; the pyrite; as well as turquoise.

Helpful items to have when activating your crystals

Items that can enhance your crystal activation process include lavender; cedarwood; nag champa incense; an incense holder; and candles or even match sticks.

Here is the simple but useful crystal activation process

- Make your setting conducive for crystal activation and energizing

    o The place needs to be somewhat dim, with only some candlelight

    o It needs to be quiet

- o Right in front of you, place one unlit candle

- o At the same front, place a stick of incense

- Sit down with crystals well held in your hands

- Take slow and deep breaths

  - o Focus on the fact that you want the crystals activated and re-energized

  - o Visualizing your crystals radiating bright light that surrounds you in full protection.

  - o You may also wish to visualize that radiant light seeking into the body of someone who is feeling unwell, and effectively clearing the entire person's hurt.

- Now make a point of lighting the candle before you using a single match

  - o Then use the lit candle to light your incense.

  - o While tightly holding the candle in one of your hands, direct your mind to focus on your intent.

- It is now time for you to visualize the flow of strong positive energies around you

  - o Begin by imagining the flow of healing or even protective energies traversing through your hand and entering the crystals you are holding.

  - o Then sweep the crystals over the candle flame as well as over the nice scented smoke of the burning incense.

- o   As you visualize the crystals taking in the positive energy from both sources, visualize its glow becoming brighter, second by second.

- Keeping your crystals well cupped in your hands, visualize their energy pulsing

  - o   At this time when your visualizing your crystal's pulse, visualize too your crystal turning to the color that is associated with your purpose and intent.

  - o   In this regard, if what you intend for your crystals is to raise your confidence, you will visualize your crystals adopting red; for protection you will visualize blue; and so on.

Now that your crystals are well re-energized and ready to discharge their role of protecting and healing you, you may wish to put them safely in your pocket or in your pouch – that is, if you are interesting in personal healing and not necessarily purifying and harmonizing an environment. However, even when wrapped or enclosed somewhere, it is an added advantage to you if you took time to touch the crystal periodically. That direct touch gets you receiving direct energy from the crystal to you.

Is that the end of the story as far as crystal re-energizing goes?

No – once in a while you could place your crystals some place where they can sap some energy from the sun or even the moon. Of course, you must consider those crystals that risk fading when exposed to strong sunshine. Those ones you can expose to early morning sunshine as it is not usually scotching. Otherwise they are better being laid out in moonlight. Some people also choose to place their crystals on the window sill for a while to get recharged by the sunlight. Do have in mind that the sun discharges strong energy whereas the moon discharges energy that is gentler. So do make your choice according to your need.

Remember Mother Earth also has its natural energy that can do your crystals a lot of good. So you may wish to bury your crystals in the soil for a couple of days to get re-energized. If outside is not convenient, your flower pot can do the trick – just bury your crystal there for, say, three to seven days.

Proper Way of Storing Crystals

If you want your crystals to retain their luster and energy vibrations, you need to handle them with care and love. You need to avoid exposing them to long periods of sunlight otherwise they are likely to get faded. Some of the safest ways to store your crystals include:

- Enclosing them in a pouch

- Wrapping them using a silk scarf

Chapter 21:
Poisonous Crystals from Unscrupulous Sellers – Avoid

In the wild, there are fruits that you do not like and then there are those that are outright poisonous. This is the same case with crystals. There are those you will not be caught dead wearing only because you deem them unappealing, and then there are those that can practically send you to your early grave. The latter are the ones you need to know so as to protect yourself and people that are dear to you and whom you may wish to buy jewelry to don.

This information is very important because in this world where people try to sell you ashes for sugar, there is no telling what con jewelers in the market may try to sell you.

Cinnabar

Cinnabar is associated with the sacral chakra and can also support the root chakra when leaning towards orange. And believe you me, in days of old, merchants would sing its praises – it brought them wealth by enhancing their creativity. Some people may tell you of cinnabar's beauty and its healing properties, but what they fail to alert you about this reddish crystal is its mercury content. This crystal whose scientific term is mercury sulfide can have mercury vaporizing and endangering people's health as environmental temperatures change. Even when it does not cause you instant visible harm, wearing or carrying cinnabar around can begin to give you tremors or even reduced sensation. Sadly, it can also end up being outright fatal. In fact, it is known to be the most dangerous of the healing crystals, being extremely toxic.

In centuries gone by, the Chinese even used cinnabar to make ornamental meal dishes. The Roman Empire prided itself in cinnabar mining because its mercury content gave it a high commercial value. Today, however, you know better than handling mercury materials haphazardly. In fact, with the rich information available, you may wish to give cinnabar a wide berth. Even some Chinese experts issued a word of caution over the use of cinnabar around 2003.

Orpiment

This crystal can do a great job of aligning your solar plexus. And you may find it difficult to resist the golden colors of the orpiment crystals. However, even with the beautiful bright yellow and orange, just in case you did not know, the crystal has arsenic in it. And the fact that the arsenic combines with sulfur to make the crystal does not make orpiment any less of a danger.

Arsenic happens to be one very toxic chemical, and the orpiment crystal can even transmit its toxicity to your body just by holding it, through its arsenic powder that has carcinogens as well as neurotoxins. This beautifully seductive crystal was once used by the Chinese on their arrows to make them poisonous and lethal to their enemies. And it is unfortunate that some ancient cultures used it mainly in ochre paint for its beauty, oblivious of the danger it posed to its user. In fact, there is no telling how many artists died from the habit of applying ochre on their bodies.

However, today, any mixture with orpiment should give itself away by the garlic smell the arsenic portion of it discharges. Orpiment is also one of those crystals that disintegrate whenever they are exposed to light.

Stibnite

The stibnite is supportive of the navel chakra. However, this crystal has an extremely unstable compound, the antimony sulfide. It may have this attractive and silvery look alright, but the crystal can easily cause death. It has already been established that when stibnite is used in cutlery, people end up suffering food poisoning and others even die. So even touching items made out of stibnite really call for instant thorough hand washing.

Torbernite

You may get excited that you have some bright ornament with prisms of blooming green, but that may just be your death sentence right there. The crystal contains the radon gas – extremely lethal to the level of causing you lung cancer! Even when they are beautiful for your table setting, give them a wide berth.

Arsenopyrite

This is another of those crystals with arsenic. Why would you wish to handle something, however gold-like, which will leave you with deadly residue in your hands? Just forget these iron sulfide crystals. You may even detect some garlic smell if you expose them to elevated temperatures.

Asbestos Chrysotile/Amphibolite

You are better off giving these crystals a wide berth in whatever form they are presented to you. They have the potential to wreak havoc on your lungs. They have silica; oxygen; sodium; and iron in them. The crystals emit carcinogens that then irritate your lung tissue to the extent of scarring.

Galena

The galena crystal is supportive of the root chakra. However, since it contains lead and sulfur, it is dangerous to have around. You may not know but inhaling lead particles over time could result in fatalities. In fact, it is one crystal that poses danger to you even as you go through the processes of clearing and energizing it. Blatantly speaking, the minute galena is extracted from underground and brought to the earth's surface, its threat to the environment starts immediately.

Hutchinsonite

This crystal that is named after the world renowned mineralogist, John Hutchinson, is more lethal than most of the lethal crystals we have already mentioned. And you cannot dispute that when you realize that the crystal has in its composition the infamous lead; the catastrophic arsenic; and then the extremely toxic thallium – pure danger you have there. Why then would you wish to endanger your life or that of anyone else just to wear or have around beautiful crystals? Sadly, the reality is that most people who acquire these crystals are least informed and just go by their attractive prismatic or needle-like shapes; or get drawn by their reddish or sometimes clear colors.

Chalcanthite

Is it beautiful? Yes – and not just beautiful but with a seductive, almost irresistible blue. But it has copper, sulfur, water, and even some other elements. The danger is that the way this combination is makes it very easy to absorb copper beyond the safe limits. Hence toxicity sets in and this can even lead to death. Chalcanthite has been known to exterminate algae in water ponds and that tells you what its capability is even to the larger environment – not pleasant.

Coloradoite

The discovery of this crystal in recent years brought smile to mineralogists – but it happens to be a compound of mercury telluride! Mercury is dangerous. Tellurium is extremely toxic. What then does their combination become? Deadly, for sure! And even having the crystal within an area where temperatures are likely to rise means you will be risking inhaling the deadly vapors released.

And whereas information is power, ignorance can be deadly. Years ago, when Australians within the Kalgoorie area learnt that some parts of their roads had had their potholes filled up with a mineral that usually comes out of the earth's crust with gold sediments attached – tellurium – they reinstated those potholes fast, this time on a larger scale. They dug out the fillings trying to see if they could become overnight millionaires from the any gold in the mix – and chances are that the greatest job was done with bare hands.

Chapter 22:
How to Identify a Reliable Therapist

Do you realize how dangerous a free-for-all market can be? Of course, there is the positive side of giving the consumer a wide range of choice, but there is also the risk of having some quacks taking advantage of the ignorance of product users and service consumers. Just as in any other trade, the field of alternative healing could do well with some form of regulation or moderation. Of course, not many countries, if any, can speak of formal regulation as far as the field of crystal healing and associated therapies is concerned. However, some countries have, at least, encouraged practitioners to have some kind of self-regulation. The UK is a case in point.

How does self regulation help?

For one, birds of a feather fly together. So when working under an umbrella body, practitioners can easily address the challenges affecting them. Those challenges may include flagging quacks who may be giving the healing trade a bad name. It may also include highlighting who their affiliated members are, therapists who would not shy away from being interviewed or questioned about their practice. That is the kind of self regulation that gives potential clients confidence in particular therapists.

Of course, in countries where practitioners of complementary and alternative medicine (CAM) are also qualified medical doctors, such as in Germany, you would not need to worry about the level of knowledge of such therapists. Then there are other countries, such as the US where you find around half of the therapists being qualified medical doctors, but without much regulation for the remaining half. In fact, beyond herbal treatments and chiropractic, many of the other forms of alternative treatments are not addressed by many governments. When it comes to chiropractic, US mainstream regulatory bodies have long recognized the practice and it is even covered by insurance.

How does the UK regulate the practice of crystal healing?

First of all, there is the *General Regulatory Council for Complementary Therapies* (GRCCT). This is the national body that maintains the register of practicing complementary therapists. If you want to know the recognized therapists in the country and for how long they have been in the trade, this is the place to seek relevant information. You will also be able to find out if any one of those you are seeking has a history of malpractice or not.

The birth of GRCCT began with the UK government encouraging practitioners of alternative medicine to form associations with a view to rooting out unscrupulous therapists. This was because, although there has not been laws regulating these practices, the government knew there was need to protect the public the same way it does when it comes to consumer goods and mainstream practice of medicine.

Essentially, what happened was that each discipline formed its own professional association, and then came up with the standards, requirements and guidelines that they deemed suitable to retain a credible and worthwhile practice. Eventually, those are the professional associations that then came under the federal body, GRCCT.

It is important to note that being in the federal register – the one maintained by GRCCT – means also that you meet the patient safety standards of the National Cancer Action Team as set by the National Health Service (NHS).

Disciplinary Action

In case you are a practitioner in an association under the GRCCT, any complaint against you as a therapist is analyzed and debated within the structures of GRCCT. In case you are found wanting, you are deregistered from the national list of recognized therapists. That is a great way of keeping potential clients from your clinic. Since the complaints section of GRCCT is very robust, individual practitioners endeavor to observe the Code of Professional Conduct & Ethics, which is great news for the public. Registered practitioners even make a conscious effort to invest in continual professional development.

Advantage for the Registered Professional Therapist

Whether your practice is based solely on crystals or you have Reiki and crystals working together, you are at a personal advantage when registered under GRCCT. Just as in mainstream medicine, there is the risk of being accused of professional negligence or such other malpractices, and you can go down both professionally and personally if you have no shield. Luckily, when you are in the national register maintained by GRCCT, you enjoy professional indemnity and you have public liability insurance as well.

Body Maintaining Standards of Crystal Healing

As far as the discipline of crystal healing goes, practitioners also have an avenue to maintain high standards by undertaking training courses offered by a credible body. Some associations of crystal healers came together back in 1988 and

149

formed a single body with common interests – the Affiliation of Crystal Healing Organizations (ACHO). Their main aim was to promote training as well as competence within the field of crystal healing. ACHO operates under the Crystal Therapy Council (CTC), which is a body registered under GRCCT. In fact, CTC was officially acknowledged by GRCCT as the lead body as well as professional council representative of the crystal healing discipline at the end of August 2011.

As far as keeping abreast with discoveries and knowledge on crystal healing therapies, the ACHO has taken up the challenge of establishing schools where new entrants as well as veterans in the trade can keep updated. This is a great way of ensuring further protection of the consumer and elevated standards of practice. For any crystal healing school to qualify under the ACHO, it is evaluated by the CTC for its quality of training as well as management standards.

It is also great news to note that crystal therapists who reside outside the UK can also benefit from the schools founded in the UK. There is, for instance, the International Association of Crystal Healing Therapists (IACHT) that offers part time classes that continue for a period of 2yrs. The course that is set to cover 12 weekends was originally designed by practitioner, Hazel Raven, and it was later modified by practitioner, Sue Baron. IACHT itself was established in 1986.

Chapter 23:
Are You Clinking Glass Or Crystal?

Travelled or not, you do know that people have a custom of celebrating great achievements with champagne or other valued alcoholic drink, don't you? And what do they serve such drinks in, as drinking vessels as well as for the purpose of clinking in cheers? Well, they serve such drinks usually in wine glasses or, alternatively, the crystal. And how do you tell when people are clinking crystals from when they are clinking wine glasses? Truth be told, a good number of people won't be able to tell the difference. And even for those who know the difference, a casual glance may not suffice. Just by mere look, the difference is very subtle.

How is the crystal really different from the glass?

Here are the different aspects where the two differ:

- They vary in chemical composition

- They vary in thickness

- Their clarity varies too

- Each is cut differently

- The refraction varies

- Each sounds different from the other

- They are different in weight

And since you are certain there is a different side to crystals than cheers and celebrations, it is imperative that you are able to tell the difference between crystal and glass. Otherwise you may find yourself spending a fortune on eBay or even in a conventional store buying stuff at a high price in the name of crystal, only to realize it is not the valuable material you thought it was.

But what, exactly, is glass?

Through the chapters, you have come to appreciate what crystals are and so any mention of something made of crystal is relatively easy to imagine. What you may want to know clearly is what constitutes glass. Simply put, a glass is that drinking container that is made out of glass. Oh... made of glass! And what brings it close to crystal then to warrant comparison?

Well, if you consider glass as raw material, it is basically soda lime. In fact, most glasses in today's manufacturing are made of soda lime. And if you analyze further, you will appreciate that you are referring to raw material that is not pure in composition. It is made up of soda and lime, and also silica. Soda, for one, is a form of mineral – sodium carbonate. Lime itself is some alkaline substance you get after the process of heating limestone. It is actually some white caustic material. And when it comes to silica, they are actually pieces of the mineral, quartz. Aha! And quartz is a known natural crystal. This crystal forms simply as silicone dioxide. It is colorless and not reactive. It is also hard material. From this explanation, it cannot be difficult now to fathom how glasses from authentic glass can be confused with containers made of crystal.

Of course, in everyday use you will find items of ordinary glass being used or displayed commonly as light bulbs; window panes; figurines; and, of course, as drinking vessels. And this is contrary to items made of natural crystal, which are normally used as ornaments; decorations; as well therapeutic products. Needless to say, glass is much cheaper than crystal.

Here are different types of glass for comparison

Borosilicate Glass

This material also goes by the term, Pyrex. Its composition includes silica; boric acid; soda and other substances. The material is non-corrosive and also heat resistant, the main reasons you will find it being used often in laboratories.

Fused Quartz

How you derive this kind of glass is by heating original quartz crystals at extremely high temperatures until they melt. And here you derive the kind of glass used to make laboratory equipment; high-end cameras; as well as halogen lamps.

Crystal

Whenever someone asks you to bring out the crystal, usually after some good news has been aired, you know that is reference to the elegant glasses made of lead oxide; silica and soda or even potassium carbonate, which is often referred to as potash.

And why would crystal be valued over ordinary glass?

Well, one obvious reason you may be able to pick out easily is the presence of elements that are made from original crystal like quartz. And besides that, crystal as a drinking vessel is valued:

- Because it is durable

- It is beautiful to look at

Why call drinking vessels crystal when they are not made of pure crystal?

Good question that needs to be addressed lest confusion remains regarding crystal glasses... This has a historical angle to it.

It all emerged from the Italian community. Italians valued glassware from their island of Murano in Venice, the place that led Europe in producing crystalline glass for many centuries. The glassware in Murano was so valued that the country protected related local skills in all ways possible. Just so you know how precious Italy felt their glass products were, anyone caught leaking the process of making the Murano glasses was threatened by death.

Of course, it is difficult to contain the spread of craft as people are always travelling, and so in due course the craftsmanship was replicated elsewhere. Still, for their wares to sell as well as those made in Venice, the glassmakers passed them as 'cristallo'. So anyone imitating the original glasses of Murano called the product *cristallo*, the English equivalent of crystal. This was because the wares from Murano were as eye catching as crystals.

In short, when crystal refers to the precious drinking vessel, it does not imply that the vessel is made of material that is a product of crystallization – at least not solely. The material may be almost as radiant as crystals, but it is just a mixture of different materials; with no purity of content like natural crystals, and with no definite arrangement of ions and molecules like natural crystals.

So, no – you cannot break your crystal after a drinking session and have yourself some healing pieces. The molecules for this particular crystal are not spatially aligned and they do not have regular patterns that have repeated themselves over years of crystallization. Mostly what manufacturers do is add a percentage of lead oxide into the mix, which has the effect of raising the glass' refraction index – science at work and marketing at the fore!

Chapter 24:
Do You Know The Top Priced Crystals?

Much as crystals are used for healing therapies, there is nothing wrong with having a beautiful crystal playing a duo role – that of healing as well as that of enhancing beauty. In fact, there are many people who buy crystals in form of jewelry singularly for their aesthetic value, only to realize the crystals have healing properties just as a matter of coincidence. Sometimes crystal buyers want to know the price tag of various crystals just in case they have occasion to buy one for someone close.

Here are some of the top priced crystals in the market

The Red Diamond

You could tread the globe for months on end before you come across this valuable crystal. In fact, this crystal that is associated with the crown chakra is the rarest of all known crystals. The pieces that can actually be said for sure to be red diamonds cannot even exceed thirty in number. No wonder then their market price is around the staggering figure of $1,000,000 per carat. Talk of a hefty price!

Incidentally, this is not a theoretical analysis by any measure. There is evidence that Sotherby's put on the market a 2.26 carat red diamond back in 2007 and someone bought it at a whopping $2.7 million! You are right to put that at $1.18 million per carat.

Grandidierite

This rare crystal that transmits light in varying colors – green; blue; and even white – is almost exclusively found in the island of Madagascar. It is one of the rarest gems and goes at a market price of around $20,000 per carat.

Jadeite

This crystal that does exemplary well when paired with the 4th chakra, which is actually the heart chakra, was said to have preceded all other gemstones. Its going market price is in the range of $20,000 per carat. It may not be very surprising that the jadeite goes for such a high price, because in addition to being a rare gem, it is also associated with great virtues – of mercy; modesty; courage; valor ; as well as wisdom. And when it comes to healing, the crystal is not just good in dealing with fatigue and strengthening your immune system, it is also linked with improving the function of the kidney.

The ruby

This famous and popular brand of red sapphire sells at a much higher price than other varieties of sapphire. And even the ruby itself has types and the most pricey one is the *pigeon blood ruby*. The ruby is associated with your base chakra and its going price is around $15,000 per carat.

The Diamond

The diamond crystal may not be as rare as many of the crystals already mentioned, but its price is just as mind boggling – going for around $15,000 per carat. The reason for the high price of this crystal that is associated with the crown chakra is its great popularity. Diamonds come in different shades, some being more expensive than others. Red and white top the list of colors in being expensive.

Paraiba Tourmaline

This crystal, named after a Brazilian state where it was first identified, is associated with the heart as well as the throat chakras. Its most outstanding features that may contribute to its high price include its distinct and stunning combination of colors which include turquoise; aqua; blue; and even green. Would it surprise anyone then that the crystal is referred to as the Peacock Stone?

Incidentally, the discovery of this precious crystal is relatively recent – just 1989. And the man who did the world of beauty and healing the great favor by identifying the crystal in Paraiba was Heitor Dimas Barbosa. From then on, man's desire to identify other crystals as beautiful as the Paraiba Tourmaline was insatiable. And the work of geologists and other experts was rewarded when, a few years later – 2003 and 2005 – they discovered similar crystals in Mozambique as well as Nigeria respectively. The Paraiba Tourmaline has a market price of around $12,000 per carat.

Alexandrite

This magnificent color changing crystal is associated primarily with the heart chakra. However, it also enhances the working of both the crown as well as brow chakras. Its market price is around $10,000 per carat. It is important to note that this crystal is becoming popular by the day, especially in the Asian countries of China and Japan. What that implies is that the price of the alexandrite crystal is likely to shoot up.

Bixbite

This is one crystal in the family of crystals referred to as the Red Beryl. This set of crystals has its origin in the ancient

Mesopotamia, where people actually worshipped it, referring to it as a magic stone. It may interest you to know that in this same family is the aquamarine; emerald; goshenite; heliodor; as well as the morganite. Bixbite is associated with the heart chakra as well as the sacral chakras.

Make no mistake: Bixbite is not *bixbyite*. The latter is an independent mineral while bixbite is the crystal alternately named the red beryl. In colloquial use, you may hear someone refer to it also as the red emerald. The market price for this precious crystal is around $10,000 per carat.

The Emerald

You cannot confidently speak of the emerald being in the category of rare gems, but its price still remains high. What is the reason? The first reason is obvious – its popularity; meaning that there is always great demand of the emerald crystal in the market. The other pertinent aspect is how difficult it is to cut emerald to a saleable piece. Its market price is generally around $8,000 per carat. The emerald crystal is associated with the heart chakra.

Musgravite

This rare crystal that is associated with your brow chakra sells for around $6,000 per carat. The name, Musgravite, is linked to the place the crystal was first discovered, Australia's Musgrave Mountains. The discovery of this gem that comes mostly in green and also violet was made in 1967. Something to note is that the Musgravite can easily be confused with taafeite, another rare crystal discovered in 1945. It is likely that not only the beauty of this crystal makes it expensive but also its rarity. But for some Musgravite found in Madagascar and Tanzania, there is not much of it in the market to write home about.

Sapphires

This crystal that is famed to have been worn by wise King Solomon of the Bible as well as good old Father Abraham, still of the Bible, is associated with wisdom, royalty, and things divine. It is used to great effect in stimulating both the throat chakra as well as the third eye.

It is important to point out that sapphire comes in varying hues and it follows that the price of the crystal varies accordingly. You have got the black sapphire; the green sapphire; the orange sapphire, otherwise known as the padparadsha sapphire; pink sapphire; violet sapphire; white sapphire; and also the yellow sapphire. Whereas some of the sapphires sell at a couple of hundreds of dollars per carat, there are still others whose market price is in the range of $4,000 and $6,000 per carat.

Benitoite

This is one crystal you may not come across anywhere but in the state of California in the USA. It was officially taken note of in 1907 in the county of San Benito, hence deriving its name from that place. When it comes to this purple-bluish crystal, size is of utmost importance. When dealing with a tiny crystal, you may be able to acquire it at, say, $500 per carat; whereas when dealing with sizeable crystals, the going price is in the range of $3,000 and $4,000 per carat. The benitoite crystal is associated with your third eye.

Poudretteite

This rare borosilicate crystal was officially discovered in 1987 in a place called Mont Saint Hilaire within Quebec in Canada. It actually derived its name from the name of the family that run the quarry where that discovery was made. This crystal that comes in varying colors – pink; purple; and even colorless – is also found in Burma. Its market price is around $3,000 per carat.

Demantoid Garnet

This crystal whose popularity is clearly rising is often referred to simply as the demantoid. It comes in distinct green color and is associated with the heart chakra. As in other precious crystals, the price may be relatively low for a single carat crystal than for a bigger sized crystal. In this regard, you can find a small demantoid crystal selling at around $2,000 per carat, then in the rare moments of dealing with a 5-carat crystal, the price shoots to even $6,000 per carat.

Black Opal

This is another precious crystal in the same price range – around $2,000 per carat. You may be able to find the black opal in Australia without any strain, but its popularity has made its price to keep on rising over the years. Sometimes the gem market is volatile and you can find that whereas you have some black opals going at the price already mentioned, some of those black opal crystals whose quality is just average are selling at just a couple of hundreds of dollars per carat. On the other hand, those of exclusive quality can even sell for around $5,000 per carat.

Taaffeite

For pronunciation, say *'Tar-fight'*. Taaffeite is a crystal associated with the crown chakra. It was officially discovered by Count Edward Taaffe, hence the name of the crystal. Curiously, the count did not discover the taaffeite crystal in a mine or amidst freshly dug minerals. He found it attached to a spinel amidst a lot he had bought. That was back in 1945. The selling price for this crystal is around $2,000 per carat.

Blue Garnet

This crystal that is also great for the base chakra comes in a fascinating color change pattern. The ones with the most profound color change – switching between bluish, red and even purplish – are the ones that are most pricey; going also at $1,500 per carat.

Jeremejevite

This crystal that is associated with the base chakra is one of the rarest. For its rarity, it is priced very highly, with its light blue variant being the most expensive. The crystal derives its name from the Russian mineralogist who discovered it in 1883. And its name is actually not pronounced the English way but *'ye-REM-ay-ev-ite'*. What makes the jeremejevite crystals that are available in the market all the more expensive – in the range of $1,500 per carat – is that out of those few thousand crystals of jemerevite found, just a handful can be cut into saleable gemstones.

As you can see, there are many variables that come into play when determining the price at which a particular crystal is going to be offered for sale. For art collectors, there is no telling how high they can drive the price of a crystal that they want; particularly in an auction. However, for those crystals that are mainly used for the purpose of healing, their prices are fairly stable. In fact, a good number of healing crystals are quite affordable and within reach of the average buyer.

Something else worth noting is that not all information that would help to determine the real price ranges is available. For one, a good number of the precious and rare crystals have exchanged hands over the years under private arrangements. As such, nobody but the concerned parties gets to know the magnitude of the financial transactions taking place. In short, the prices given in this chapter are general pointers and not figures that are necessarily exact and on point.

Chapter 25:
Comparing valid facts with Myths and Folklore

All work without play... Yes, brings boredom and dullness, alright. And here you have done nothing but learn the great facts of crystals; information that can transform your life from one of popping pills to one of natural healing and wellness. In which case you now qualify to take a break and have a good laugh, as you marvel at the myths and tales that used to surround these beautiful items of nature.

Although fascination with crystals was there amongst people in the olden days just as it is today, the tales told about these pieces were often far-fetched and sometimes even ridiculous. Of course, it is easy to visualize the ancient Roman Emperor Nero, as it was said of him, watching his gladiator games through a massive piece of emerald! He had power, didn't he? And he also was royalty, or wasn't he?

Got your hanky in your hands now? Ok – it is break time and you can let go and laugh out loud if you wish; or rather, if you can't help it.

- In Romania, what did they say about you possessing a chrysoprase crystal? Well, essentially that you and the lizard could chat one on one – basically you understanding the language of reptiles!

- According to the Greeks, the amethyst crystal is actually a beautiful virgin girl turned statue by the powers of goddess Diana who saved her from the jaws of two tigers unleashed on her by an irate god Dionysius. And its purple colors are the stains of god Dionysius' tears that he shed in remorse afterwards.

- The labradorite is said to have fallen right from the skies landing along the Labrador coast. And there is talk about an Inuit warrior hitting the rock severally in an attempt to release the lights apparently trapped within it; but he only managed to release some of it.

- As for the Hematite, Native Americans as well as Romans believed in its power to make them invincible in times of war. The Native Americans painted their faces with it as red ochre while the Romans used its powder after crushing it to rub it onto their bodies.

- And tourmaline...? Once upon a time, so the Egyptian tale goes, this rock was traveling from the Earth to the Sun. Along the way it came across the rainbow and happened to brush against it, thus collecting all those colors that it now possesses.

- As for the Golden or Imperial Topaz, it was commonly believed that it could alter its color if put within the vicinity of foodstuff that had been poisoned. And the crystals were, therefore, used to protect royalty. In fact, that is where the reference *Imperial* Topaz came from.

- Then with the quartz, many believed that it was actually water that gods had frozen eternally and then released to the earth from the heavens.

- Then there is the sunstone which many believed was a genuine part of the sun that broke off and fell from the skies during one of those full solar eclipses.

- As for the pearls, you were so sinful – the human race – that the angels up in Heaven shed plenty of tears in sorrow. And then...? Those tears happened to land onto the sea, entering gaping oyster shells.

- According to the Australian Aborigines, God once came to earth aided by the rainbow (He really needed that assistance!) And where he happened to land His feet is where the opal appeared.

- Ancient civilizations had it that the earth sits on a humongous piece of sapphire. Now, this sapphire is the one that radiates all the blue you see high up in the skies.

- You know the Black Obsidian? The Mayans looked at it the way you would a piece of polished mirror. And what did they come up with? They claimed to see right into their future!

- And during medieval times, topaz was said to make you invincible whenever you wore it.

Conclusion

If you choose to partake in a crystal healing exercise, know that you may be exposed to long-lasting energy shifts. While the changes may be startling to you at first, the effects are beneficial, and you will eventually learn to recognize and enjoy the feeling of the natural cleanse and restoration that your body, spirit, and mind have achieved.

While you don't need to perform a full crystal healing all the time, it may be beneficial to do so when you're feeling particularly sluggish or have been exposed to a strong source of toxins, pollution, or negativity. It is also refreshing to know that healing crystals are safe for expectant mothers as well as children. In fact, considering that expectant mothers are normally advised to avoid unnecessary medication, having alternative therapy in form of crystal healing is a godsend.

As you continue to practice crystal healing, you'll develop a greater sense of balance within your own body, and you'll be able to pick up on any of your chakras becoming discordant. You can then choose to rein in on that chakra specifically, placing a crystal nearby the affected area so as to bring it back to its optimal frequency. Oftentimes, you may just wish to wear certain crystals on your body or have them around your dwelling place to maintain a healthy balance within yourself as well as between you and your environment.

Crystal healing is a holistic, easy, and harmless way to balance the mental and physical systems of your existence. If you are still skeptical about the practice, we encourage you to give it a try and start slowly. Even if you begin only by using a quartz crystal, which has many balancing benefits in itself, you can ease yourself into the practice in a gradual way.

It's important to allow your mind, spirit, and body to be open to the practice of crystal healing. Remember that your being is not solely made up of one plane alone; rather, it is an entire entity that combines your mental, emotional, physical, and spiritual capacities. Disease, ailments, and general uneasiness affect you on each of these levels; thus, each aspect must be treated and balanced, instead of focusing on the physical aspect alone. By achieving harmony across each of these realms and balancing your chakras, you can attain a long-lasting sense of ease, confidence, and bliss.

In fact, you may be able to tap into the powers of the supernatural, using relevant crystals to help you connect with your spiritual guides and angels. You can then understand yourself better and subsequently create a healthy environment for yourself. When you know how to use the right crystals, you will even be in a position to protect yourself from negative energies that mar your spiritual energy flow making you susceptible to disease.

Thank you.

REIKI FOR BEGINNERS

The Complete Guide To Supercharge Your Energy And Reclaim Your Health By Unlocking The Power Of Reiki !

L. Jordan

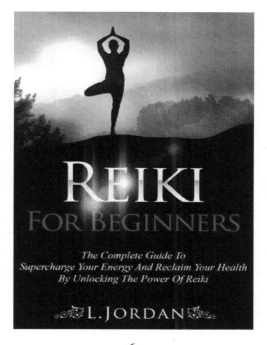

Table of contents

Introduction

If you are like many, you may have heard of Reiki and been interested in it, but do not know where to start. There is a lot of information out there about the healing energy of Reiki and how it can help you but a lot of that information is for those who are already trained in the art or Reiki master's. Sometimes you just want to start at a beginner level and get yourself familiar with the concept before going into the complexities of something. This book is aimed at helping you do precisely that. Within the pages of this Reiki book you will find information on what Reiki is and how to put some basic and helpful techniques to work for you. Reiki is an amazing force and when used properly can help with a great many things such as:

- Relieving stress.

- Treating depression and anxiety issues.

- Balancing your emotions and finding better self - esteem.

- Balancing your center to help with insomnia and overall fatigue.

- Releasing pain.

- Healing for a general feeling of well-being.

- Helping overcome past trauma or grief caused by PTSD, sexual trauma, emotional abuse or physical abuse.

- Reduction in the side effects from medications.

- Help in living with chronic pain or other chronic issues.

- Improving your overall health and immunity to germs.

- And more, there are very few limits on what Reiki can be used for.

Chapter 1:
What is Reiki

The word Reiki is made of two separate Japanese words - Rei and Ki. When we translate Japanese into English we must keep in mind that an exact translation is a formidable undertaking because the Japanese language has many different levels of connotation. Therefore the context the word is being utilized in must be kept in mind when endeavoring to communicate its essence. Because these words are utilized in a spiritual rejuvenating context, a Japanese/English dictionary does not provide the depth of designation, we seek, as its definitions are predicated on prevalent everyday Japanese. As an example, Rei is often translated as a ghost and Ki as vapor and while these words vaguely points in the direction of designation, we seek, they fall far short of the full definition that is needed.

When seeking a definition from a more spiritual context, we find that Rei can be defined as the Higher Astuteness that guides the formation and functioning of the cosmos. Rei is a subtle sagacity that permeates everything, both animate and inanimate. This subtle sagacity guides the evolution of all formation ranging from the unfolding of galaxies to the development of life. On a human level, it is available to avail us in times of need and to act as a source of guidance in our lives. Because of its illimitable nature, it is all powerful and knowing. Rei is additionally called God and has many other names depending on the culture that has denominated it.

Ki is known to many as an energy that is within all life. It is not something that can be touched in the sense that it is not solid or physical, but it is there and it gives all of us life. Ki has a flowing property and moves through humans, animals and plant life, it can be found in anything that is alive on the planet. When you have a good amount you feel strong, energetic and motivated. Someone with High Ki is ready to take on any challenge that life may have for them throughout the day. When you have a low amount of Ki you are going to feel run down, weak and chances are you will pick up any little sickness going around as well. Ki can be gathered from fresh air, good food, the warm sun and getting an ample amount of sleep. Other-ways for to improve Ki include breathing routines and meditation. At the time a person passes away the Ki that was with them leaves their body and goes to other places within the earth. Ki is also considered the Chi in Chinese mythos, the Prana of India and Ti or those from Hawaii. Throughout modern history it has also been referred to as bio plasma and life force.

With the above statements kept in mind you can then give Reiki a firm definition that it is a non-physical or medical form of healing that uses life force that is being led by a higher intelligence or that it is life energy being guided spiritually. This working definition works side by side with the life experience of those Reiki Masters who use the Reiki energy daily. They report that Reiki seems to have a mind of its own and that it will ebb and flow as needed, pouring more energy into the subject who needs it and work to form a condition that will heal what needs to be healed. Reiki cannot be guided by mind control which is a benefit in several ways, it allows the energy to not be limited by the experience of the practitioner and it can't be used in a harmful way. Simply put Reiki is a healing energy and only a healing energy it can never do harm. Reiki is more complex than a simple life force energy which can be used to do harm and be influenced by the mind, Reiki is pure healing life force energy and you should always keep that in mind when using it.

175

Ki that moves throughout the body is the source of the healing good health, energy it is also Ki that gives the organs and tissue of the body life and animation, this is what creates good health within the organs and throughout the body in general. When the flow of Ki is blocked or somehow interrupted the organs and tissues in the body will be affected in a negative way. It is the lack of Ki and free flowing movement of that Ki that most often causes illness of any kind within the body.

An important piece of Ki and understanding how it flows in understanding that it will respond to your thoughts and feelings. Ki will flow well or diminish to a trickle depending on your thoughts and feelings on any given day. It is negative thoughts and feelings that will weaken the flow of Ki throughout the body. While western modern medicine might not fully subscribe to the thought of Ki as a force in the body, they do recognize and state that around 98% of illness is caused directly or indirectly by the brain and how we think about something.

It must be clearly understood that your full mind does not only live in your brain. In fact the mind lives through-out your entire being. As anyone who is even slightly knowledgeable about anatomy knows the nervous system extends to every organ and bit of tissue in the body where the mind and therefore Ki extends and can flourish. Every person also has a small field of energy around them outside of their body that is called your aura and the mind and your Ki extend to this as well. When you look at it this way it becomes apparent that you should call your mind and body simply the mind because it is all interconnected.

Now that you know this it is easier to see why negative thoughts don't just reside in your brain, but they spread out into the body and even the aura and begin to form pools. It is these pools where Ki becomes restricted and unable to flow. When these pools are located near organs they become deprived of Ki and function becomes restricted. If negativity does not quickly become removed from the mind and brain serious illness happens.

When negative thoughts are more subconscious than conscious a greater problem occurs. When you are not aware of the problem you don't know it is there and can have trouble changing your mental outlook or eliminating the thoughts all together and that is where the value of Reiki comes in. Since Reiki is guided by the Higher mind it knows where to go and how to tend to the problems and pools of negative energy in order to unrestrain the flow of Ki to a specific area. It will work with the conscious part of the mind as well as it does with the subconscious so eradicate anything that is harming the flow of Ki throughout your body. As Reiki works through an unhealthy or ill area, it will break up the negative pools of thought or feeling and allow the Ki to begin to flow normally again. Once the Ki begins to flow at a healthy pace the areas that were under nourished become well fed once more and illness is chased away to be replaced by good health.

Reiki is a noninvasive form of healing that is gaining popularity because of the fact there is no harmful chemicals, drugs or surgery involved ad it works. Western medicine is moving forward and studying the effects of Reiki on patients and we can look forward to seeing it become more commonly used as they see the positive results practitioners already know about. In conclusion to the question what is Reiki, the simple answer is that it is a form of natural healing that uses the body's own Ki to cure illness. Moreover, in the next chapters you will learn how to heal with Reiki and make yourself and your loved ones happy and healthy the natural way.

Chapter 2:
Reiki principles and symbols

Before you can begin any form of Reiki healing you must know the basic components of the system of healing that Reiki uses. There are five basic elements that are utilized whether you are healing yourself or another. Keeping this list handy will ensure that you are always prepared to give or receive Reiki healing.

Attunements: Also known as initiations when used in Reiki healing this is known as being in tune with the energy. Being in tune with Reiki energy guarantees that you will be able to channel the energy properly.

Hand positions: These are important in Reiki healing and involve knowing where to put your hands during the healing. They can be split into two forms, treating yourself and treating others.

Meditation: The easiest way to focus with the Ki in the body and preform Reiki healing is to meditate or focus on the energy within yourself.

Symbols: Use the symbols of Reiki were needed and use the sound their name makes as a mantra when you need to connect with the energy.

Reiki Principles: There are give basic principles to Reiki healing and they should be used daily as a source of encouragement and during meditation before you heal yourself or another.

Now knowing this basic list and always keeping it handy in your mind, or even in a print off, we need to look at some of the concepts more closely. The first and most important are the five principles of Reiki:

Principle 1: *For today, I will not be angry I will focus on goodwill*

When you have a focus of anger or upset whether it be at yourself, your loved ones or what is going on in the world you create blockages in your energy. It is the biggest and most complex of the inner demons we all battle with. Reiki is the right tool to remove those blockages caused by anger. These pools can be accumulated over a short period of long period and still be removed. While Reiki can remove the pools it cannot remove the source of anger. Letting go of your anger will bring peace into your mind and energy.

Principle 2: *For today, I will not worry*

Like anger, worry causes blocks, but worry tends to stem more from future events. The more worrying that we keep in our minds, the more pools and blockages it can cause. Where anger needs a focused Reiki healing to undo, worry needs the energy to be spread throughout the entirety of the body and mind. When you let go of things and stop worrying you bring healing to your body.

Principle 3: *For today, I will be grateful*

Be grateful starting with your heart and spreading throughout your entire body. Small things count, such as smiling at someone, offering kind words, showing gratitude and giving thanks. These small things all count and when you are thankful you bring joy to your soul.

Principle 4: *For today, I will do my work with truth*

This means to support yourself and your family in a way that does not bring harm to other living beings. Earn a living, but do so in a respectable way, make sure your life is lived with honor. Working truthfully will bring love to the will of mind and body.

Principle 5: *For today, I will be kind to anything that lives.*

Bring honor to your family, by being kind. Show kindness to all things great and small be they human, animal or plant. By being kind you bring more love into the will of the mind and body.

The next important tool in Reiki is knowing the symbols, they are considered sacred and some are not revealed until your second or third level of mastery. For the purposes of this book, as a beginner to Reiki there are just a few basic ones to know, and use as mantra.

ChoKuRay

Said: choh
koo
ray
Also called: "The symbol of Force"

Means: Deity and mortal being coming together

This symbol is most commonly employed to directly increase the power of Reiki it will draw energy from around the healer and will go where you focus it. To use it you will make the sign over yourself or the person you are healing and silently say the word Cho Ku Rei 3 times.

- This symbol is one that can be employed anytime for anything. Including:

- Emergency treatments

- Treatments done at once with little preparation

- To clean an area of negative energy

- For protection of the spirit

- To cleanse food, drinks, medicine and herbs of negative energy.

- At the hospital for healing

181

- To give more power to other symbols

- To seal in healing energy that has been placed for treatment.

SeiHeiKi

Said: say
hay
key

Also called: The symbol of the mind and feeling

Meaning: The opener of the universe

This symbol is most commonly employed in healing that involves cerebral or sentimental problems. It is good to calm the mind and is also best used for:

- Protection against physic attack

- Mental cleansing

- During meditations

- For balancing both sides of the brain

- To aid in overcoming addictions

- Healing trauma

- Aligning the upper chakras

- Removing negative energy

HonShaZeShoNen

Said: Hanh
shah
zay
show
nen
Also called: The Space Symbol

Meaning: The deity within me greets you

This symbol is employed in distance Reiki healing. You will draw and use it when you wish to send healing energy to anyone that isn't directly in a room with you.

TamAraSha

Said: Tam
ara
sha
Also called: The Harmony Symbol

This symbol is employed to bring balance and harmony to the body and soul and will also strengthen Reiki energy being used to bring down a blockage. It is used commonly for:

- Grounding energy

- Balancing energy

- Unblocking energy especially, at chakra centers.

- Used over painful areas to reduce or completely do away with the pain.

The final item from the list that is used overall is attunement. In general a deep attunement can only be done for you by a Reiki Master, so if you plan on a full attunement or going deeper with your Reiki practices than a beginner level you should consider finding a Master who can attune you.

However, there are basic steps that you can do as a beginner to attune yourself.

Step 1: Sit in a place that has no distractions, soft music can be played and prepare yourself as if preparing for meditation. Center yourself.

Step 2: With your right hand draw the symbols of ChoKuRay, SeiHeiKi and TamAraSha on your forehead.

Step 3: Visualize your chakra's and the energy that radiates from them. Follow that flow outward and through your body and aura. As you visualize chant the three symbols, names quietly three times.

Step 4: Lightly touch your forehead again, the third eye and visualize the constant flow of energy, balance and how you can share that energy with others to heal them or heal yourself.

Once you feel you have centered yourself enough and have a firm grasp on your own inner Ki, you are attuned on a basic level and can preform the beginners Reiki healing that is in the next chapters.

Made in the USA
San Bernardino, CA
12 September 2016